Called to be Men

What Our Western Culture Has Stolen From Men

Steve Heimbichner

Called to be Men: What Our Western Culture Has Stolen From Men

Copyright © 2019 by Steve J. Heimbichner

ISBN:

A Gift Just for You!

Please read this first!

Just to say "Thank You!" for buying this book, we would like to give you a special video teaching 100% FREE.

Honor:
The Language of the Bible
with Pastor Steve Heimbichner

TO DOWNLOAD GO TO:
www.elccmt.org/c2bm/

Dedication

To Yeshua the Messiah, who in every season and circumstance, is my great Rock, Deliverer, Redeemer, King, Shepherd, Teacher and Friend. He is YHVH, "the Hand who Holds Existence Together".

To all the Godly men that have spoken into my life over the decades…my grandfather, father, uncles, brothers, friends, teachers, and mentors.

To Evelyn for her support and encouragement in the process of writing this book and creating the Called to be Men study course.

To Everlasting Covenant Congregation in Billings, Montana for simply being the spiritual family of Messiah that makes spending the Sabbath together a treasure.

ש

Numbers 6:24 – 26 (CJB)
(Hebrew and English)

Y'varekh'kha ADONAI v'yishmerekha.
[Yahweh will bless you and keep you.]

Ya'er ADONAI panav eleikha vichunekka.
[Yahweh will make his face shine on you and show you his favor.]

Yissa ADONAI panav eleikha v'yasem l'kha shalom.
[Yahweh will lift up his face toward you and give you peace.]

Foreward

The trickster's first attack was on the headship of man. Since then every generation of men has struggled to find their place in who they are created to be as The Holy Man/High Priest of their home. In today's society technology has replaced traditions that marked the beginning of a man's life through a time of testing and ceremony. *The Called To Be Men* book and program is fresh living waters for men across the spectrum of churches to learn how to be men and fathers of their house according to the ancient biblical principles that are applied to each individual for their edification and growth.

On the Northern Cheyenne and Crow Reservations, the CTBM program was started after Creator brought three ministries together in unity and the success is incredible. Pastor Steve and his team have ministered with humble hearts and outpouring of love to First Nation men who are receiving the teachings and growing into the mighty men of Yah that they were created to be. This program is helping to transform reservations that had lost hope in so many ways and is now experiencing a revival within the men that are then taking it to their families and communities.

Chief Joseph RiverWind
FireKeepers International First Nations Ministry
Peace Chief - Northern Arawak Tribal Nation

Table of Contents

Introduction:
The Call to be Men

Okay, men, I know what you are thinking. "Why should I read this book? What's going to be in it that I haven't heard before? I really don't need another guilt trip on not being a real man." Many of you, like me, have done the Promise Keepers thing, sat through dozens of Father's Day sermons, listened to hours of family-help radio and watched instructional DVD's with our spouses telling us how to have a better marriage.

Likewise, many of you, like me, have walked away inspired and ready to make big changes in our lives. Yet a couple months down the road, the inspiration has waned, the changes that we so readily pledged to undertake are forgotten, and our resolve has faded away. Why did this happen? What went wrong?

Men, we have been honest enough with ourselves to acknowledge that we are not real sure what we are doing. We know our culture and society is in desperate need of good men, husbands and fathers. We desperately want to be these men. Yet, after all the great material and motivational get-togethers, we still feel clueless on how to rebuild ourselves, our families, our communities and our nation. If you are like me, you have felt let down and sometimes helpless. The self-talk kicks in. "What is wrong with me? Am I really that screwed up?"

I promise you, this book is different. It will take you beyond inspiration and motivation. It provides truth and instruction that goes beyond tips and challenges. No guilt trip involved – just honest understandings and empowering good news. This book is about rediscovering God's long established Biblical pattern for becoming a man and showing you how to walk in that pattern. It provides not only knowledge, but the purpose for you *as a man* that is behind that knowledge. God made you. He knows the plan He has for you – one filled with success and good. He has created a perfect path for you to walk in the amazing journey of becoming not just a good man, but an extraordinary man. He has also established a way to pass that path on to your sons and grandsons.

My Challenge: to get you to read this book. Let's be honest. Very few everyday men actually sit down to read a book. Most guys claim they lack the time to read. Some have poor reading skills and avoid it. Others simply do not enjoying reading. I appreciate it when these men honestly tell me they would rather hear a sermon, listen to a CD, or take a course of instruction. I encourage them to find a method that will open their lives to the wealth of good instruction found in books for any area of their lives. A couple of my buddies have become so motivated to learn that they now ask their wives to read books to them. It's kind of a "couple thing" – something they can do together. I admire these men. Not only did they take initiative and responsibility for gaining instruction they knew they needed, but they chose a means that requires guts. They actually wind up talking to their wives about what they have read together. Now that is courage!

Courage is exactly what is needed and now is the time. We are at a serious crossroads in the culture and society of the United States. Nearly 25 million (36%) of our children live in fatherless homes. These children comprise 63% of youth suicides, 93% of homeless children, 85% of children diagnosed with behavioral disorders, and 85% of our youth in prison. Yet, it is not just these children (and their mothers) that we need to be concerned about. There are millions of children with their biological father in the home, yet he is emotionally and spiritually absent from their lives. Dad knows he needs to be there, but hasn't a clue how to be a good dad or a good husband. Confronted with the enormity of the void, he instead throws himself into work or sports or anything that he can figure out how to do well in and personally prosper.

The result is heartbreaking. Our children are not healthy and happy. Far too many are lost and confused. They are looking for security, direction, validation, and blessing from a father that is no longer there for them. In anguish, they seek for these things elsewhere and the path they take often leads to their own destruction. Is this really our fault, men? Did we receive any of these things from our own fathers? Unfortunately, most of us did not. Very typically, neither did they.

Dare I say it? Both the abandoning father and the clueless-but-still-at-home man are just plain scared. We should be. Our own misgivings are terrifying in themselves. In addition, we are bombarded by the endless voices of talk shows, music videos, magazine and internet articles, sermons, conferences and idle conversations at work. All of these voices are giving their opinions, ideas and instruction on being a real man, husband and father.

How do we know who is right?

To make matters worse, there is a huge void of good role models via the entertainment industry. The Simpsons, Family Guy, American Dad... Come on – give me a break! The non-animated versions of "family life" aren't much better. Are you serious, America? It's as if we've given the men in this country license to be idiotic, self-absorbed, inconsiderate, obnoxious and virtually incapable of providing wisdom, love, and guidance to their families. I can't even watch these programs. They turn my stomach and grieve the Spirit of God within me. As I look at the men around me, both in and outside of the church community, I see increasing confusion and a deepening fear of failure. Ignorance and apathy are acceptable counterfeits that have lulled us to sleep. It's as if we've accepted failure as the new "normal". **Men, it is time to wake up!** In our current culture, guys, we are being set up to fail. Thus, a call to courage! We can succeed as husbands and fathers, if we *choose* to.

Yet I must give you warning. The call to be men as Yahweh designed is a journey to *Biblical* manhood that depart from cultural and church traditions. It takes bold steps and dedicated resolve to finish this journey well. Are you up to it? Are you willing to put everything you thought you knew about being a man up for review? Are you willing to scrutinize your own belief system and seek out truth-filled answers to your questions? Are you willing to let down your defensiveness long enough to consider that Western Christianity just might be missing some of the answers it promises to provide? Are you courageous enough to evaluate what you believe and why? Have you the guts to weigh out if what you believe is truth or well-intended deception?

The prophet Jeremiah recorded for future generations (that's us) an interesting statement of direction given by God to His children. **"Thus says the LORD: 'Stand in the ways and see, And ask for the ancient paths, where the good way is, And walk in it: Then you will find rest for your souls.'"** (Jeremiah 6:16 NKJV) This is an amazing promise. God himself instructs us to ask for the ancient paths as they are good paths. He promises us that when we walk these paths, we will find rest for our souls. Peace. Purpose. Completion. Confidence. We can know what we are doing is true and right. I know that is what I want in my daily life. I imagine that you do to.

What then do we need to do? According to God himself, we need to walk in His ancient paths. Herein lies step one to becoming an extraordinary man. You and I need to find out what His "ancient paths" actually are and how they can be walked out today. We need a blueprint we can rely on; one that has been tested by generation upon generation throughout time.

The most basic of the ancient paths God is referring to is simply called the Torah. Some call it the "Law". Jews call them the Principles and Instruction of Yahweh, often very simply "The Path". In the days of Moses, the Hebrew people understood the instructions found in the Torah to be their Wedding Covenant. What we call The Ten Commandments are the Wedding Vows of that covenant. At Mt Sinai, God, the King of the Universe, pledged Himself to them. Israel, the nation He called out to be His Bride, responded with a heartfelt pledge of, "We will". In return, Yahweh promised to bless them, care for them, and always be with them.

The Hebrew faith has always in its very heart understood that the Mt. Sinai experience was not a loveless God handing out a heavy law. Rather this was a loving God taking a Bride called Israel and choosing to dwell on earth amongst all the nations through His marriage to Israel. His goodness revealed to the nations that through their relationship, this would be how He would call all mankind to return to Him. Paul teaches that when we receive the Messiah, Yeshua (Jesus), as our Savior and King, we become grafted into the same Covenant. Through uniting ourselves with Messiah, we become sons of Abraham, Isaac, and Jacob (whom God renamed Israel). We are citizens of the set apart nation He calls the whole House of Israel.

Israel's Wedding Covenant with God has become ours, including its Ten Wedding Vows. The intimacy of God dwelling in us and His goodness to His Bride continues to testify to the world. Through that testimony, He continues to call all mankind to return to Him. This marriage is an ancient and eternal covenant God seals in blood more than once; the blood of a Passover lamb in Exodus and the blood of the Passover Lamb in Matthew, Mark, Luke and John. Such a strong covenant can never be broken.

Yet the Torah is much more than a western concept of "Law" or the Hebrew concept of "Wedding Covenant". The Torah contains principles and instructions on how to be a man – a Real Man – spoken straight from the very mouth and written by the very hand of the Creator that fashioned man and breathed life into him. Yahweh is His name. (Exodus 3:15 "YHVH") In ancient Hebrew, the name means "the Hand that Secures Existence". That Name has spoken clearly. "The Hand that Secures Existence" has provided for His people the ancient path to a full and purposeful life. We have His perfect design to become real men living under His Reign in what is His Kingdom (not ours). Can it possibly get any better than this? No guessing. No excuses. No confusion. Peace for our souls – and for our homes and communities – are found in this Ancient Path. Hope and deliverance for our nation will come through those men who are courageous enough to embrace who they have been called by the Creator of the Universe to become.

However, it is if and only if we as men choose to walk in that path. The King of the Universe has laid the path before us in His Word and through Yeshua (who is His Word lived out perfectly in a real man). There is no mystery here. Our purpose from the very beginning of mankind's existence was to rule and reign on earth in His Name. He is our Supreme Sovereign. His desire has always been to dwell on earth with His creation – mankind – and be our God and we His people. He created us in His image and He wants more than anything for life on earth to be as it is in Heaven. The earth was created to receive His Kingdom. We were created for the purpose of establishing His Kingdom on this earth.

Unfortunately, the first Adam gave all of this away to our enemy, Lucifer. Praise God, through Yeshua, whom Paul calls the second Adam, it all belongs to us again! The challenge to each of us is whether we will step up to our purpose, gentlemen (and ladies), take up the Principles and Instruction of His Kingdom, pledge ourselves anew to our King (who is also our Groom) and live like the people He created us to be. He tells us how. This Kingdom does have a "Constitution".

Some call the constitution of Yahweh's Kingdom the Torah. Some call it the Pentateuch. Some call it the "Five Books of Moses". Regardless, if you are courageous enough to do your own homework, you will soon realize that every other book in the Bible beyond those first five (including the New Testament) revolve around the Torah, refer to the Torah and depend on the Torah for their very deepest meaning and truth. Without it, nothing of the Bible makes sense, including the death and resurrection of Yeshua. In it, we find the very essence of our lives.

I firmly believe and have witnessed in my own congregation that men, when presented with something they can truly sink their teeth into – this "Call to be Men" based on the Ancient Path - know immediately in their heart and gut that it will work. They simply need a little inspiration or motivation. Then they go after it with gusto. Their lives change. Their marriages improve. Their homes change. Even their church changes.

The men are suddenly "present and engaged"; in their marriages, their families and the congregation. It is not because they have to, but because they suddenly want to. They have discovered who they are supposed to be and how to live that out. The assignment fits them well. And, it should. They were made for it.

From the very beginning, Yahweh designed a man to be the foundation of the family and the family to be the foundation of community life. From the very beginning, humankind's enemy, Satan, has been out to destroy men and families. In our culture today, we see many women, in both single parent and traditional homes, carrying the role of family leadership. This is so completely reversed from what Yahweh intended in His Kingdom on earth. As I talk with women in my congregation and circle of influence, I can't help but notice that women who love Yahweh are attracted to men who love Yahweh and are dedicated to following Yeshua. These women who have become so accustomed to leading are actually bone tired – weary from carrying a load they were not designed to carry. They are tired of men who remain immature and trying to "find themselves". Gentlemen, allow me to exhort you. These women want to be rescued by purpose filled, real men of God. Rest assured guys. There is hope! No matter your age, Yahweh's purpose for your life will begin to come to the surface as you begin to obey the principles that He gives us in HIS Word – the Torah – the Ancient Path. I have seen this to be true over and over again.

The Principles and Instruction of Yahweh provide the very purpose and direction we as men so desperately need. From the Torah, we can identify "Ten Characteristics of a Real Man." Take a good look at them. I think you will be amazed at the extent of their application in our lives as men, husbands, and fathers. They answer the cry of our heart for guidance and instruction. More importantly, they are the call of Yahweh to our current generations, here and around the world.

In our congregation, we have developed a nine week course for men entitled **Called to be Men**. What you are about to read is the book version of this course based on my notes and live instruction. Take your time going through this material. Allow Father to sink it deep into your mind and heart. I pray that it will empower you, as it has many others, to step forward and courageously begin to change your life. I assure you, the adjustments you make will positively change for the good the lives of your family for generations to come.

Some of these changes will require sensitivity on your part in how you implement them into the life of your family. Don't rush your household. Answer their questions. Share with them why you are implementing changes. Show them what you are learning. Some family members will resist. Give them time to adapt. Be aware that these are Biblical truths that much of our culture has forgotten or rejects, even within the church. True, lasting change takes time. Don't give up! Be diligent and ask Yahweh to help you. He will, as He is the one longing the most deeply for you to be all that He destined you to be. He is firmly on your side – for your sake and for the sake of those you love.

Gentlemen, I applaud you for your courage to answer the call to be men. With the great crowd of witnesses in Heaven above, I cheer you on as you run your race to win!

> *My people are destroyed for lack of knowledge.*
> *Because you have rejected knowledge,*
> *I also will reject you from being priest for Me;*
> *Because you have forgotten the law of your God,*
> *I also will forget your children.*

Hosea 4:6 (NKJV)

Ten Characteristics Of A Real Man

You will show me the path of life; in Your presence is fullness of joy; at your right hand are pleasures forevermore.

Psalm 16:11

1. **A Real Man desires to know and love Yahweh** (God, called by His name).

   Messiah confirmed that to love Yahweh with all one's heart, mind, and soul is the greatest instruction in Scripture. (Deuteronomy 6:5) As in any relationship, to love deeply requires communication. A man must have communication with his Creator at all times. This communication is called prayer. Prayer changes a man's perceptions about his life. This in turn changes his understanding of the circumstances he is facing and allows him to see an opportunity or the new course of action Yahweh is putting before him. Prayer also opens the door for God's wisdom to enter a man's thinking. A man who prays sees results. Such a man learns to trust Yahweh the moment he begins to feel overwhelmed. He knows that his source of true strength is found only in Yahweh.

2. **A Real Man seeks to build Yahweh's image within himself.**

   Obeying the Torah brings a man in order with Yahweh's thoughts and character. This man knows that obedience to HIS ways will bring tremendous character, knowledge, self-esteem and self-confidence to his own life. Such a man realizes that while the Spirit of Yahweh brings deeper relationship with his Creator, the Torah teaches him how to walk in responsibility. Choosing to walk in responsibility keeps him steadfast in the Word of Yahweh and gives him a standard to live by and to pass on to his children.

3. **A Real Man desires to build up the gifts and talents that Yahweh has given to him.**

   This man is not lazy with what Yahweh has placed in him. He works to develop his skills, educate himself, and walks with mentors. He discovers that even the mistakes he makes while building his unique set of gifts and talents cause his character to become deeply developed and defined. He learns how to take responsibility for both his successes and his failures. His work aligns with his purpose in life, revealing who he truly is and bringing him great joy and fulfillment.

4. **A Real Man honors his wedding vows and his family above his own desires.**

   Yeshua (Jesus) is man's example of a True Family Man. A Real Man understands that just as Yeshua does everything for His Bride to ensure that she is cared for, protected and honored, he also must do the same for his own wife and family. The well-being of his wife and family comes before his own desires and enticements. Yeshua went so far as to die so that the fullness of a complete and blessed life would be made available to His Bride, the children of God's Covenant. A Real Man will do all that he can to provide that same completeness and well-being for his wife and children.

5. **A Real Man lives out the community principles found in the Torah.**

   Yeshua confirmed that the second greatest instruction in Scripture is to love others as oneself. (Leviticus 19:18) A Real Man sees to the care of the needy in his congregation and community. He guards the lives of those not able to guard themselves. He stands for the ways of Yahweh in the "city gates", which are the places of leadership and influence in his community. He seeks justice for the wronged, yet extends mercy as the Torah instructs.

6. **A Real Man walks out his faith by actions.**

   He proves his beliefs by what he does. He is known as an encourager. He is steadfast in his trust of Yahweh and does not worry. He builds faith, not fear, into the lives of others. He gives of his possessions to those in need while diligently caring for his family. He speaks blessings over the lives of others. He is a faithful participant and servant in his congregation. He listens to and obeys the instructions and statutes for the full scope of his daily life given by God in His Word.

7. **A Real Man brings out the best in others, especially his own family.**

   As a father, he trains his children in the ways of Yahweh in such a manner so that when they are older, they will not depart from them. He does not provoke anger and resentment within them. He helps his wife and his children achieve their potential. He believes in himself and builds self-esteem and self-confidence into their lives. He shows love to his family openly and embraces them joyfully.

8. **A Real Man understands the necessary balance between justice and mercy.**

   He is compassionate yet fair. He knows when to be firm and when to be gentle. He extends forgiveness, yet does not set himself or others up for harm. He knows the difference between an insincere "I am sorry" and true repentance. He pursues becoming both a good priest and a good king in Yahweh's Kingdom on earth.

9. **A Real Man is faithful to build the Kingdom of Yahweh.**

   He cares for the poor, widow, fatherless, and orphan. He is a tither and a giver of offerings. He works to bring healing and restoration to the lives of others. He equips himself with knowledge of the Truth and shares that Truth with the lost ones in this world. He is a Light to all those around him living in darkness and can help them find their way into Yahweh's kingdom.

10. **A Real Man is a student of the Word of Yahweh.**
    He studies Scripture to deepen his walk of obedience to his King. He knows the times and seasons of Yahweh's Kingdom. He constantly seeks greater wisdom and understanding of Yahweh's principles and instruction. He watches over his family by leading, teaching, and guarding them so that they are able to recognize the world's deceptive ways and resist assimilation with them.

Gentlemen, a Real Man discovers and accomplishes his true purpose in life only by following Yahweh's instruction and principles as found in the Torah. To know the purpose of a thing, one must ask the one who created it – not the thing he created. Purpose is found only in the mind and design of our Creator.

The question of your personal purpose is unanswerable by any other man or woman. A man will find his full and unique purpose only when he seeks out and asks his Creator. Personal peace, growth and confidence will come only when he agrees, in heart and action, to pursue Yahweh's answer.

Chapter One:
Becoming a Man of Godly Character

The call to be men in the Kingdom of Yahweh has all the earmarks of royalty. Everything a Kingdom man says and does should reveal four magnificent Kingdom virtues: courage, integrity, fidelity and honor. What images do these words conjure up in your imagination? I can think of several: a soldier, a knight in a king's realm, the leader of a strong nation, the perfect CEO for a major corporation. How about a fantastic husband and father?

Can these Kingdom virtues be said about you? After all, according to Scripture you are one of Yahweh's priests and kings; part of a Holy Nation set apart by Yahweh to represent Him and have dominion on the earth. (Genesis 1:26; Exodus 19:6; I Peter 2: 5-9; Revelation 1:6) Have you grasped the Biblical truth that in His sight *you are royalty*? In fact, that is exactly what you were created to be. You have a royal destiny as a king and a priest that will one day be completely fulfilled as you rule and reign with Messiah on this earth for 1000 years. Are you preparing for your destiny? If not, it is definitely time to begin!

I know that as a man I'm still a work in progress. I am diligently working out the day by day reality of my salvation, just as you are. My goal is to become like my Savior and King, thus fulfilling Yahweh's original design for me: to be fashioned in His image. (Gen 1:26) Yeshua's lifestyle is nothing less than Father's beliefs, thoughts, and character lived out on earth. His existence as King of the Universe is saturated with courage, integrity, fidelity and honor. Everything Yeshua does and says begins with the Father's Word and flows out from the heart of who the Father is. Yahweh's character and His Word directs Yeshua, and Yeshua never violates either. For this reason, Yeshua could and did proclaim that "I and the Father are one." As men of His Kingdom, it should be the same with us.

Character virtues like courage, integrity, fidelity and honor are words that can be easily spoken, but are rarely understood. If they are to be our Kingdom character goals, then we need explore these four virtues and find out what they are. A basic understanding of them is crucial to grasp from the get-go, because they will be the character traits that we need to develop in ourselves in order to fulfill the royal lifestyle He is calling us to walk. These are not "gut instinct" traits and actions. These deep virtues are chosen and developed character traits that will result in bold, Godly actions.

These strong character traits are so significant to Yahweh's Kingdom that they literally define the difference between life and death, between authentic faith that pleases Him and men who are just being religious. To develop them within you requires chosen changes in your heart, mind, and actions that will be seen by all those around you, especially your wife and children. Let's consider each trait one by one.

A Man of Courage

Be strong and of good courage, do not fear nor be afraid of them; for Yahweh your God, He is the one who goes with you. He will not leave nor forsake you.

Deuteronomy 31:6

I stated in the introduction that to be a Real Man in Yahweh's Kingdom takes courage. What is courage? Webster defines courage as: **"that quality of mind which enables one to encounter danger and difficulties with firmness, or without fear, or fainting of heart; valor; boldness; resolution."** This definition teaches us a great deal about courage that we as Yahweh's men need to understand. Courage is emphatically a "quality of mind". That brings up a fundamental and extremely important question. What is the quality of your mind these days? Who are you listening to? How are you conditioning your mind to think and respond to any given situation?

Yeah, I know. "Think." Did I have to bring up that nasty word? Yes, I have to. I have to because this is so very crucial. The quality of the thinking that goes on in our minds, men, is the key to having courage. Look at that definition again. Let's rephrase it a little so you can see the picture it presents. **My quality of mind, what I meditate on and have chosen to believe as truth, is what enables me to act with resolve in any encounter with difficulty or danger, in spite of what may be intense fear.** Courage means I can act quickly with valor and boldness because I don't have to hesitate and think twice. *I have already made my choices before the challenges manifest.* I know what my response will be. I know what to say, how to react, and what I am willing to give up my life for. My mind has been disciplined and conditioned with truth – Yahweh's Truth. I am prepared for anything.

That, men, is the definition of courage. It is not an emotion or a mystical quality some of us have and others do not. Courage is a choice. Courage is cultivated. Courage is the result of disciplining and conditioning your mind. This is why the strongest man in the world can faint in a time of danger while a ninety-eight pound weakling can become the hero of the day. Courage is not about physical strength or even great military skill. Courage literally begins in the greatest battlefield of all time, your mind.

This now begs a question. Men, are we disciplining and conditioning our minds? I know men who spend hours every week disciplining and conditioning their bodies. What if we put that kind of effort into doing the same with our minds? To become men of courage, we need to. We have some choices to make on how we spend our time and for some of us, making the right choices will be harder than for others.

I encourage you to take an honest look at what you are doing with your mind. What voices are you listening to? What do you read? What television programs and movies are you watching? Do you study Yahweh's Word for yourself or do you wait for someone to spoon feed you once a week? Have you made every effort to seek out Truth for yourself or do you simply take someone else's word for it? What do you believe? Why do you believe it? Do you take all of your thoughts captive and conform them to what the Word of Yahweh says about you or your situation? Have you chosen the standards you are going to live and die by? Will it be the Principles and Instructions of the King of the Universe, or the deceptions and lies being presented as "truth" in the world's systems and religions (including by many popular churches and preachers). Satan's deception of Adam and Eve began with a question. "Did God really mean what He said?" To cause us to alter Yahweh's Truth is an ancient, evil ploy.

As I stated earlier, ignorance of Truth is no longer an option, men. We are in a time in human history where the stakes are too high to stay ignorant or allow others think for us. Nor can we afford to remain complacent by not acting on Truth once we have found it. Ignorance undermines our ability to be Yahweh's men of courage.

The challenge to become men of courage is an age old human dilemma. As Israel prepared to cross the Jordan River into the Promised Land, Yahweh (through Moses) took them through a complete review of everything He had instructed them to be and to become as His nation. Then He presented them with a choice. It is the same choice we are facing today. Yahweh, through Moses, spoke directly to them saying, *"I call heaven and earth as witnesses today against you, that I have set before you life and death, blessing and cursing; therefore choose life, that both you and your descendants may live; that you may cling to Him, for He is your life and the length of your days;"* (Deut. 30:19-20 NKJV) Simply put, on the very day that they left the wilderness behind them, Yahweh called on His people to be courageous and choose life by clinging to Him and all that He had taught them.

Leaving Egypt (salvation/deliverance from their bondages) was behind them. However, there would be many more and greater challenges ahead. To fulfill their destiny and purpose, they would face battles to win and life-threatening conditions to make their way through. It would take trust in Him and the choice to take courage to do what would have to be done to "get there". It still does.

When the war is won in the battlefield of the mind, then the war can be won in the battlefields of life. Courage becomes action. It must become action. You can tell me until you are blue in the face what you say you believe, but until your actions reveal your beliefs, until you take courage and do something, your beliefs mean nothing.

My good friend, Jack Hightower, wrote these words to me in a recent email. They are absolutely true. "Courage is action. Action in spite of reluctance, or fear, or doubt of personal adequacy. Action in the face of overwhelming odds, insurmountable obstacles and possible and probable injury. Courage is to act to stem the tide, overcome Goliath, save the lady on the subway tracks, to take a bullet for your friend, to sacrifice your life for the name of Christ, to stand against the bully with the weakling, to care for the needy and less fortunate. Courage is to do the right thing and the right thing is given to us by the instructions of God. Courage is to give and not always take. Courage means we do not live for the here and now, but live for the tomorrow of our children's children. We live not to bring glory to ourselves, but to bring glory to our Redeemer and Savior who in giving Himself for us, asks us to give ourselves for others. Courage means it is not about me."

A Man of Integrity

To determine to be a man of courage is just a portion of our journey to becoming real men. Another key virtue of Yahweh's Real Man is integrity. Some of you are going to be surprised to discover that there is a strong spiritual dimension to integrity that you may not have before considered.

Let's go back to the dictionary again. The first meaning of integrity, according to Webster, is **"the state or quality of being entire or complete; wholeness; entireness; unbroken state."** Furthermore, Webster informs us that integrity means the subject (that would be us) is **"unimpaired, unadulterated, or in genuine state, in original condition and purity."**

Whoa! Hold the horses back, gentlemen. How many of us can say that we are in a state or quality of being complete, whole, entire; in short, unbroken? I can honestly say that I do not remember a day in my life when I have remained 100% unimpaired, unadulterated, or in the genuine state that my Creator intended for me! Men, we have been in a broken and impaired state since the fall of Adam in the Garden of Eden. And it is not just our sinful nature that makes us broken.

Life is a messy battlefield. We all have areas in which we are seriously damaged and broken. We need healing not only spiritually, but emotionally and often physically as well. If we are to be men of integrity, we must find our way back to being the men Yahweh created us to be. What I find ironic is that we as broken men go to other broken men to try fix our brokenness. This will never work. Our broken state can only be repaired by the power and hand of the One who created us in the first place. Once we have walked through His restoration process, we can go back to the beginning with Him and allow Him to teach us how to be men.

How does our Creator restore us to His original design? How do we regain a state of integrity? What does the process look like? Our first step to being restored is not that difficult, yet we make it difficult because of pride. We are men. We hate to admit we've made mistakes. It takes courage to swallow our pride, come humbly to our King and admit our screw-ups and failures. In religious language, this action is called "confession of sin". As simply as I can state it, this means that I take full responsibility for my failures and agree with Yahweh that I am broken and need to be restored to that original, pure condition He intends for me.

Then we have to repent. All too often, we confuse confession with repentance. They are not the same. In Hebrew, repentance is the word "teshuvah" and it literally means "to return". Agreement and owning up to the truth that I am broken and have failed is not enough. Yeshua never taught that all we need to do is fess up (confess) to what we did wrong. He did tell us, *"Teshuvah [Return], for the Kingdom of Heaven is at hand [drawn near, as in 'right before your very eyes']."* (Matthew 4:17) **Return!** My apologetic words will not be enough. I have to do something. I have to make a choice and a commitment. *I have to return to something.*

What am I supposed to return to? Once again, Yahweh tells us through His prophet, *"Ask for the ancient paths, where the good ways are..."* We are to return to the ancient ways of His Kingdom upon this earth: the Principles and Instructions of Yahweh. I have to return to a firm resolve (an element of courage) to walk this lifestyle of His Kingdom. I have to return to the covenant relationship man was in with Yahweh from the moment He breathed His life into him. I have to return to the ways of the covenant Yahweh made with us as His holy nation of priests and kings. Without this return (repentance), there can be no true integrity in a man. Our genuine state, found in Genesis 1, will remain completely out of our reach. Our brokenness will remain our tragic state though eternity.

This is exactly why "the Good News of the Kingdom of Yahweh" is such GOOD NEWS! At that very moment in our lives when confession *and* returning walk hand in hand, we can joyfully accept His gift of a fresh start. That fresh start is called "forgiveness" and our forgiveness was bought with a great price. That price was the death of Yeshua the Messiah. He became the final and great sacrifice that atones for man's failures and shortcomings. This is why He died. In that very moment when I confess my failures to Yahweh and choose to return to His path of Life (repent), the blood of Yeshua's sacrifice does away with all of my failures *forever*. Yeshua makes a way for us to become a real man again. Our integrity is fully restored! I bet most of us have never thought of integrity in this light before.

Interestingly Webster's second definition of integrity is **"moral soundness; honesty; freedom from corrupting influence or motive."** Now that is more like what most of us thought integrity meant. I find it very interesting that Webster put this *second* to the first definition above. Isn't that the reverse of what humans normally attempt? Most of us, I would hope, try to be morally sound and honest; making every effort to keep ourselves free of corruption. However, how many of us readily deal with the fact that we are broken beings incapable in our own strength of true integrity?

In truth, many of us actually deceive ourselves into thinking our failures are, for some reason, acceptable. (Even King David made that mistake regarding his affair with Bathsheba and the murder of her husband.) We choose to delude ourselves and deceive others by giving every appearance of moral soundness and being honest, uncorrupted men. Then when caught in a moral failure or a lie, we are so very quick to "take responsibility" for our actions and confess only because we were caught, not because we truly saw the error in our ways. It is the way of our current society to be "sorry" only when one is caught in a failure. That is not the way of the Kingdom of Yahweh.

A man of true integrity then is one who readily deals with his own brokenness and gives himself over to being restored to his genuine state by the God who made him. He confesses, returns to Yahweh's path, and receives his King's forgiveness the very moment he personally becomes aware of "missing the mark" (definition of "sin"). He does not wait until he is caught in his failure. He says far more than apologetic words. He makes the situation right and makes some personal changes, even if no one is watching.

Such a man is quick to repent (to turn his thoughts and actions around and return to the King's Path). His purity is completely restored. So is his purpose and character. He no longer lives a life of false integrity as a religious or self-righteous man who tries by his own efforts to appear morally perfect. He has become an unimpaired man who loves his King and chooses to obey His commands. The journey to fulfilling his destiny may have become a bit more complicated and challenging due to the consequences of his failures, but he can still get there! He has become a true man of integrity.

Men, when our moral integrity is being daily fashioned by Yahweh's Principles and Instructions, our daily lives become consistent with what has transpired within us. Such a man has nothing to hide and lives without pretense, fully able to be true to who he is no matter where he is or who is watching. Because there is no longer anything within him or in his lifestyle that prevents the King of the Universe from always being with him, he can, with great courage, do whatever His King commands him to do. This is an enormously powerful state of being, filled with tremendous potential. The good news is that it is entirely possible for us to walk in that state of being. All it takes is a choice, followed by sound action.

Courage and Integrity are most definitely companion virtues. Together they shine brightly in a man of moral soundness who has disciplined and conditioned his mind, is readily courageous, and fully able to act upon His King's command. This Real Man is now also becoming a man of great Fidelity.

A Man of Fidelity

Nevertheless, when the Son of Man comes,
will He really find faith [faithfulness] on the earth?

Luke 18:8

We have a good number of former military in our congregation that I have grown to love and admire with all my heart. They challenge me with the depth of their ability to follow through on commitments and readily serve others. Our former Marines are especially a constant reminder to me of "Semper Fidelus", the US Marine Corp motto that means "Always Faithful". This is exactly what our Father is looking for is us!

"Fidelus" is the Latin word that gives us the word "fidelity". Like many men, I used to think of fidelity only in reference to marital faithfulness. That was until I met and got to know Dan (not his real name). His training and service with the Marines raised a resolved standard of fidelity before me and many in our congregation that has broadened our understanding of faithfulness. Dan has embraced fidelity as a part of his life in way that most of us have never considered. He did so when he figured out what the word actually means, and he figured it out long before the rest of us.

Just in case you need to be reminded, it is imperative, men that we know what we mean when we use words; especially words that refer to our own character and lifestyle. Therefore, we take another trip back to Webster. (We are disciplining and conditioning our minds!)

Here we find that "fidelity" means **"faithfulness; adherence to right; careful and exact observance of duty, or discharge of obligations."** I like the definition found in the American Heritage Dictionary even better because it expounds on the nature of faithfulness a little more. **"Faithfulness or devotion to a person, a cause, obligations, or duties" that holds strong "correspondence with a fact or truth".**

For a Real Man in the Kingdom of Yahweh, fidelity is much more than remaining faithful and devoted to your wife. In fact, fidelity is what holds the Kingdom of God together because it is tied directly to Truth. Fidelity gives the Kingdom power and hope. Let's break this concept down so we can see the full picture.

Fidelity is faithfulness, and faithfulness means "full of faith". Faith is a good place to start because if you've been in the Kingdom of God for even just a short time, you know that *"without faith it is impossible to please God."* (Hebrews 11:6) That said, we had better know what faith is!

To do that, we need to know what that word means in its truest Biblical form – Hebrew. *Emunah* is the Hebrew word for "faith". Emunah is much more than an intellectual belief or a spiritual warm, fuzzy energy. In Hebrew, "faith" is an action word – a verb, not a noun – and it means "obedience in action". In other words, faith is not merely adhering to a belief system nor is it some sort of conjured up spiritual quality that will make something happen. Faith or emunah, is walking out what you believe. To be full of faith, or faithful, means that your life is full of action that is firmly based on what you believe.

No wonder James could write *"Thus also faith [in Greek thought, "beliefs"] by itself, if it does not have works, is dead...Show me your faith [beliefs] without your works, and I will show you my faith [beliefs] by my works."* (James 2:18) Faith must work. Faith must produce. Only then is it the true faith that pleases Yahweh. He is pleased with a man's faith when his beliefs manifest as obedience in action. Yahweh does not hesitate to do remarkable things through and around that man.

Fidelity, our faithfulness, is more than fulfilling an obligation or the keeping of a contract by our actions. Fidelity has to be tied to something we firmly believe in. Fidelity implies such a strong belief in something or someone that you willingly devote yourself entirely; not merely intellectually, but actively. In other words, it is not enough to pledge fidelity and devotion to a spouse, family, your nation, a cause, or set of beliefs (no matter how lofty they may be). Fidelity means you are actively involved in doing whatever it takes to support, supply, encourage, and guard what you have pledged yourself to. For a Real Man, fidelity means "full engagement"! Semper Fidelus! *Always faithful! Always involved!* We are to be *men of action* in our marriages, with our children, in the community of believers, and in our personal relationship with God.

Let's get personal once again, men. Look at the relationships that you have committed yourself to – your wife, children, parents, job, your walk with the King of the Universe, and your relationship with your church and pastor. How is your fidelity level? Have you measured it against and firmly tied it to the Truth that you say you believe? Are you walking out in your relationships what you claim you have committed yourself to, or just giving your intellectual beliefs "lip service"? I'm giving you the "heads up and pay attention" right now, men. Everything that we will address as we go on in this book on being a Real Man in His Kingdom will put your fidelity to test. You will need courage and integrity to pass those tests. You will also need honor.

A Man of Honor

...for those who honor Me I will honor,
and those who despise Me shall be lightly esteemed.

I Samuel 2:30

He who follows righteousness and mercy finds
life, righteousness and honor.

Proverbs 21:21

Honor is the final of our four character virtues in the fabric of the Real Men in the Kingdom of Yahweh. Before we consider honor, gentlemen, I want to breathe some encouragement into you. Remember, this is a journey – one that takes a lifetime of walking closely with the One Real Man of the Universe showing you the way and empowering you moment by moment to become the image of Him that you were created to be.

Keep in mind that the four virtues of a Real Man are not created consecutively. It is not, courage first, then integrity, then fidelity, and then honor. Rather these virtues are being woven simultaneously and increasingly into our lives as we learn, mess up, clean up and learn some more. As each day of the journey passes, we become more courageous, more honest and pure, more faithful, and increasingly capable of honor. As we make choices, become more refined in our beliefs, and always take action on them Yahweh will remain faithful. He will complete this good work He has started in you. Therefore, celebrate every victorious step forward and every lesson learned when you stumble...and then keep on walking.

Back to honor. Men, I cannot say enough about the importance of honor. This is one of the most powerful attributes of a Godly life for both men and women that I have ever encountered. So many times in

Scripture, Yahweh instructs us to honor. We are to honor Him, honor the Sabbath, honor our parents, honor our spouse, honor our family, honor one another, honor those to whom honor is due, honor the feast days of the King…honor, honor, honor. Honor is crucial to ALL of our relationships, including those in our careers and businesses.

I am like most men. Relationships are not my strong point. In fact, relationships can be downright scary and it hurts horribly when one goes wrong. Many men avoid relationships all together – as in meaningful, deep relationships. I am not overstating anything when I tell you that learning what it means to "give honor" has helped me beyond measure with my relationships in my family, in the work place, and in ministry. I am positive it will do the same for you.

On the other hand, it is also really great to receive honor. I can't think of anyone who doesn't like to be honored, especially men. We are competitive by design. For most guys, winning is everything. Why? Because we love to be honored! We like the tournament trophies, the pats on the back, the bonus checks and commissions, the employee of the month plaque with our name on it, and the beautiful gal on our arm that "turned all the others down for me". These are all expressions of honor and they feel real good.

Yet receiving honor is not about winning a competition. Receiving honor is the reward of walking in courage, integrity and possessing the ability to honor Yahweh and other people. In other words, the greatest honor a man can receive is honor that acknowledges and rewards a life of excellence. That honor manifests from words of appreciation from our children or that special look a wife gives her man that says, "I will go wherever you go and be proud to walk by your side." That honor manifests itself when our Father the King says, "Well done, good and faithful servant".

If honor is so very key to success our lives, what exactly is it? Yes. One last trip to the dictionary! Webster gives a dozen entries under the word "honor" as a noun and four as a verb. I am not going to list them all. I think you will get the picture with just a handful. Honor defined is **"esteem due or paid to worth; high estimation; respect; consideration; reverence; veneration; a manifestation of respect or reverence; a mark of respect; a ceremonial sign of consideration; to revere; to treat with deference and submission; when used of the Supreme Being, to reverence; to adore; to worship. To dignify; to raise to distinction or notice; to elevate in rank or station; to treat in a complimentary manner or with civility."**

Let me very quickly get practical. What would a day in your life look like if you went about both your business and leisure *intentionally* honoring people? I'm not talking about only those who, in your estimate, deserve honor. I'm talking about every single person you meet in the course of that one day, regardless of what you have thought or experienced of them in the past or present.

How would you esteem and give high estimation to a co-worker? What about making an extra effort to be respectful and considerate to your wife? How would your mom and dad react if you stopped by or phoned them just to tell them "I love you" and thank them for all they have done for you? What one act of honor, kindness, and encouragement could you do for someone down on their luck that would give them a moment of dignity and hope?

How about your boss—that person that drives you nuts and you know in your gut you could probably do their job better than they can? What would you be willing to do in that one day to treat them in a complimentary and civil fashion? I'm not saying "brown nose" the boss. I am talking about genuinely looking for the positive in your boss and acknowledging it. Even a simple "thank you for hiring me" is a form of honor.

Have you, from the deepest of your heart and soul, honored Yahweh lately? When was the last time you approached Him with your prayers of gratitude, songs of heartfelt worship, and cheerful giving of your tithe and offering rather than only presenting Him with a list of your complaints, needs, and wants?

Honor is a choice to highly esteem, treat with respect, and intentionally build up others around you. Honor is an attribute that we are quickly losing in our society. Hence we have teenagers harassing the elderly on public transportation, teachers who have lost control of their students, children bullying one another, parents abusing each other and their children, employees who show little respect to their bosses, and employers who treat employees as less than worthy of what they earn. We no longer want to honor our leaders in government or other arenas in society. Nor do we want to honor those who prepared the way for our own success, including our parents. This is especially true if we somehow think they haven't earned the right to be honored. After all, "we deserve" everything we have accomplished or gained. We don't owe anyone anything, especially honor. Ironically, we seldom hesitate to point out and complain loudly about a lack of what we think we are entitled to. We are quickly becoming a nation of whiners and insulters.

I'm not sure of where to start when it comes to our present culture and instruction concerning honoring Yahweh. Even within the church community, we struggle with honoring Him. I truly believe our problem is that we have turned Him into a religious figure rather than recognizing Him for who he truly is – our Creator and King. I shudder to imagine His regard for those who take His name, His very character and authority, lightly. When asked which is the greatest commandment, **Yeshua was quick to reply, "Hear O Israel, the Lord our God, Yahweh is one. And you shall love Yahweh your God with all your heart, with all your soul, with all your mind, and with all your strength."** (Mark 12:29-30) To give everything within you in dedicated love to our Creator and King of the Universe is the high esteem He desires from us. He is worthy of our honor and deserves nothing less. Our reverence (respectful awe) of Him is to be rooted in a deep love and fidelity.

Sometimes it is easier to understand something when you consider the meaning of its exact opposite. The opposite of honor is dishonor. I want to talk to you about dishonor for a moment because dishonor is running rampant in every area our society. Just one shift in your understanding of dishonor may change your entire life. It certainly changed mine.

Dishonor means to disgrace someone, to discredit or make light of them, reproach them or cause them shame. One of the greatest dishonors is to ignore someone or not fully engage in their presence. We do that a lot in our culture. We walk past someone in the store without a word, even though we know and recognize them. We sit across the table from someone at a restaurant or at home and send texts or answer phone calls in the middle of –or sometimes instead of – conversation.

The ultimate dishonor is to attempt or actually cause a person's loss of their reputation. Just as honor builds up, dishonor tears down. Just as honor strengthens relationships, dishonor damages them. In fact, extreme acts of dishonor toward a person can destroy them. (We need only watch the news media, the conduct of political parties, a good number of politicians, and the nightly talk show hosts to get full blown examples of blatant, destructive dishonor.)

To dishonor Yahweh the Most High God means that you take His existence and His sovereignty lightly, as if it doesn't matter or carry any relevance to your life. His Word, His instructions and principles, are optional. In fact, they can be done away with. Dishonor questions and usurps His authority. Dishonor is the root of rebellion and seeks to remove Yahweh from His place of authority and sovereignty. We would rather serve on the throne of our own lives, than hear and obey what our King is instructing. The moment we think and act on that, we immediately fail in honor and fidelity to the One who we claim is our King. We give him "lip service", but our hearts are far from Him. We have answered the question, "Is He my King or not?" And our answer is "No, not really".

The worst dishonor of Yahweh is to curse Him, deny His existence, and attempt to discredit Him in every way. Such a person not only tries to "destroy God", but also tries to destroy the trust and lifestyle of those who honor Him with all their being. Those who persecute Yahweh's children – the priests and kings of His Kingdom on earth – are actually doing all they can to dishonor Him. In essence, they are persecuting Him through persecuting us. Just as Yeshua experienced, we suffer under their hatred and dishonor of Yahweh.

As a devoted and loving follower of Yahweh, you must understand that to do or speak something to dishonor Him harms your relationship with Him. That loss greatly grieves Him, and eventually it will come to greatly grieve you also. This is because dishonor attacks your very covenant with Him and seeks to destroy it. To dishonor Him would be an act of unfaithfulness and possibly betrayal. Do you see where I am going with all of this? Simply put, sin is "an act of dishonor" and acts of dishonor separate us from our Creator. We cannot accurately hear His voice from such a distance and certainly not through the fog of our indifference to Him.

Dishonor also creates destructive chaos in our relationships with people. When we break our word, when we act or speak unfaithfully, when we do something to damage or tear down another person (gossip, malicious lies, painful insults, physical violence, marital unfaithfulness) we dishonor them. We act in complete disregard of their value as a human being. We disregard any covenant we might have with them. In dishonoring them, we have sinned against them by our irreverent thoughts, words, and actions against them. In so doing, we also bring dishonor on our own lives. In fact, dishonor against others leads to our own poverty and failure. Those who dishonor not only Yahweh, but other people lose opportunities, promotions, jobs, healthy family relationships and will eventually lose their own sense of personal dignity. In other words, dishonor (sin) destroys lives...mostly our own.

When I came to understand sin as dishonor, I started to guard my actions and my words much more carefully. I now have an even deeper desire to be sinless, without dishonor, before my King. My heart's desire is to be one of His men of honor. A man of honor does not intentionally harm those around him, especially in some twisted effort to make himself look better than someone else. A man of honor gives high esteem and respect to Yahweh and to people. He respects the Creator as the source of all life and therefore he respects every human life around him. He knows that the life of every person he encounters was, like his own, put on this earth by the same Most High God that made him. A man of honor always builds up and never tears down another individual, even someone he strongly disagrees with. (Our politicians and political commentators could stand a few lessons on honor.)

Honor is exactly what Yeshua did every time He touched an unclean person, entered the home of an undesirable and washed the feet of His disciples. He understood and sought to affirm each of them for who they were beneath all the damaged goods. Did they earn or deserve to be treated with such great honor? Through the eyes of most, absolutely not. But through the eyes of the One who created them, yes they did. If He saw in them the desire and ability to humble themselves before Him, He most willingly honored them for one simple reason. He made them. He saw in them their willingness to repent (return) and He deeply wanted to help them rediscover His own image crafted within them. I am called to walk as He walked among men; therefore I can do no less.

I could say a great deal more about honor and how to implement this virtue in your life. In fact, I could write a whole book on the topic. Yet I will stop here for now because, rest assured, the topic of honor will resurface repeatedly as we make our way from here. You will quickly realize that Yahweh's entire Kingdom and our role in it is enveloped in our ability to give and to receive honor. To become a man of honor in His Realm is not an option. It is an absolute requirement.

Brother, are you stuck at a stalemate in your relationship with your wife? Do your children no longer respect you? Have you been overlooked again for a promotion at work? Are your finances in shambles? My suggestion is that you review your life carefully and look for actions or words of dishonor you have enacted toward God or another person in some place or at some time your life. Go back and make amends. At the same time, intentionally begin to honor God, your parents, your wife, your children, your friends, and your employer. Honor everyone your life comes into contact with. Hold them in high esteem. Look for the image of God within them and make an intentional effort to strengthen and encourage them. I have every confidence that giving honor will cause your life to take a dynamic shift!

Be it Resolved

God's call to the men in His Kingdom is one that has not changed since man's time on earth began. Will we choose a path of life or a path of death? Will we be men of courage, integrity, fidelity, and honor? When the heat is on, are we prepared to respond to our challenges as men who have chosen life and are resolved to follow no other way? The life of our families and our future generations depends, men, on us.

We now know what courage is. We know what it means to walk a life of integrity and fidelity. We know what it means to be a man of honor. We understand that every good thing we do in obedience to our King is at its best when it comes from a life of personal character that is being shaped to His image. I trust that you are inspired with much more than a rallying cry, but with an understanding of what that cry is all about.

You have a royal role to fulfill. You were born for it. You have a King to serve and honor. He has done everything possible to open the path of this bold life before you. The Principles and Instructions of His Kingdom have been given. Are you ready to move forward? Are you ready to choose Life? If so, join me in this pledge.

I resolve that from this point forward in my life, the four virtues of Real Men in Yahweh's Kingdom will impact and shape everything I say and do. I pledge that as I make every effort to live out the Principles and Instructions of my King, I will endeavor to do so with Courage, Integrity, Fidelity and Honor. I do this in dedicated, heart-felt service to Him. I fully acknowledge that I was fearfully and wonderfully made for this extraordinary lifestyle. I accept my King's high call...the Call to be Men. Amen! (So be it!)

Chapter Two:
Becoming a Man of Blessings

When I was a child, I spoke as a child, I understood as a child, I thought as a child; but when I became a man, I put away childish things.

I Corinthians 13:11

For those of us who are married, or have ever been married, we understand one very important concept. Before that wedding ceremony, we were single, but after that ceremony we were married!

A wedding ceremony closes the door on the life of a single person and changes their behavior and lifestyle forever. The covenant agreed to by the bride and the groom binds two lives together, not just physically but also emotionally and spiritually. Something incredible happens in that the way we think about ourselves as men changes. (The same is true for the bride.) We act differently, think differently and respond to life's opportunities, challenges, and needs differently. From that day forward there is never a doubt that we are married. We know the date of that union and remember the specialness of that ceremony. (At least I hope that you do!)

People who live together will never be able to claim such a tremendous day, never be able to claim they are married, even if they live together for forty years. That ceremony, as old fashioned as some may think, is *a day of sanctification*. It sets two people apart as one in a relationship that is solely theirs and establishes their unique identity in the community. We remember our wedding day all of our lives because that was the day our status changed. That was the day that we became "husbands".

Let me ask you a question. Do you remember the day you became a man? I'm not talking about having sex for the first time. Any boy who has reached puberty can do that. I am talking about identifying a specific day and time that your status changed from being a boy without much responsibility to a man ready to assume great responsibility. If we are being honest about men in our culture, I think we can readily agree that we know men who are still quite immature even though they are well into their adult years.

What truly makes it possible for us to shift from boyhood to manhood? I think we know that answer, guys. For a boy to become a man, he needs the validation and blessing of his father. As I have talked with men throughout my years in ministry, most are still longing to receive that. Unfortunately, our culture simply no longer has a vehicle for which this important transference of a Father's Blessing can occur.

As mentioned in the introduction to this book, through the prophet Jeremiah, Yahweh instructs us to ask for the ancient paths and walk in it. (Jeremiah 6:16) Our culture, including the church culture, has pretty much done away with most Biblical instructions that create and enhance a Kingdom culture of giving and receiving blessings (i.e. the seventh day Sabbath and the Feast Days). Perhaps one of our greatest losses in the church is the loss of knowing how to bless our wives and children. In fact, the more I come to understand the power of Yahweh found in this ancient practice the more I have come to realize just how tragic this loss is.

The practice of imparting a blessing over each other, over our spouses, and over our children and grandchildren is as ancient as it comes. In the Garden of Eden, this practice was established by The Creator himself as he blessed His children, Adam and Eve. His example was carried on through the Hebrew culture as "the Fathers Blessing" and every father and child in that culture understood the magnitude of such words.

The rite of Blessing the Children passed on from Adam to the next generations for many centuries before it surfaces in writing again through the Biblical accounts of Abraham, Isaac, Jacob, Joseph, Moses, David, Yeshua, and even in the early church. In many tribal cultures that still exist around the world today, there remains a rite of passage ceremony preceded by some type of ritual or task a boy must successfully pass through in order to be recognized by the community as a man. Yet, do we see this very important validation of the arrival of a boy's manhood in our Western culture? The answer is "no". That absence has created a huge void that college fraternities and even street gangs try to replace by hazing and other often very dangerous "rites" that teens and young men actually submit to just to prove that "I am a man".

Men, our families, and the church, are missing out on a huge service and opportunity to help our boys become men; one that the Hebrew culture still holds firmly to. To this very day the Jewish culture, which is based on the ancient Hebrew culture of the Bible, has maintained this crucial God-given principle of a Father's Blessing through a special ceremony conducted when a child reaches the age of 13. This ceremony is called a Bar Mitzvah for boys and a Bat Mitzvah for girls (Meaning "Son of the Covenant" and "Daughter of the Covenant). Because we are of Yahweh's Kingdom, we need to understand how this precept of a Father's Blessing desperately needs to be understood and restored to our lives, families and congregations today.

I want to clarify one issue that has probably already risen in your mind. The Father's Blessing is *not* a Jewish tradition. *It is a Biblical principle.* Unfortunately, the Jews have been the only ones among "Bible believers" that were wise enough to hold on to it. Thankfully, many Messianic and Hebrew Roots congregations are restoring this principle and practice to their congregations. Hopefully, the church at large will soon gain this crucial understanding also.

The reason is as simple as it is powerful. We need the boys in our congregations to "grow up" and become men who are confident and capable of successful lives governed by our Father Yahweh's principles and standards, not those of the world. We have to also be honest enough as congregations to face up to the fact that we also have grown men among us who are still acting like boys. This too can change! The good news, men, is that *it is never too late to receive, or give, a Father's Blessing*. Believe it or not, no matter when in life it is understood and received, it does make a difference.

What does it mean to bless someone? The Hebrew word for blessing is "baruch", which means "to empower to prosper". When we bless someone, especially our children, it means that we validate their importance as a human being and are releasing them to move forward in life successfully. This might also involve empowering them with a gift that would help them achieve their personal destiny. It most certainly involves speaking words that encourage, build up, and give positive direction. Blessing someone communicates an expectation. We want the person we are blessing to know that we believe in them and know that they can become all that the Creator designed for them to be. In fact, we expect them to pursue what He has designed for them.

In a Biblical Hebrew culture, such blessings are spoken over our children every Shabbat and in many homes, every day of the week. This is an incredibly empowering practice that sets our children up for accomplishment and builds healthy self-esteem. Can you imagine the confidence that builds up in a child when at least once a week he or she knows that "Papa is going to encourage and bless me!" For a child who receives their father's words and actions of blessings every day, there is not much of a chance for an expectation of failure to develop in that child's soul or mind.

What would your father's blessing have meant to **you** as you grew up? Would your self-worth and self-perception be far different than it is? Of course, it would be. Now, imagine how empowering that your "Father's Blessing" would be for your own children! For some of you reading this book, you are now being presented with a huge opportunity to turn your family history completely around and dramatically change the lives of your children, grandchildren and beyond. I cannot stress this enough. Family curses will be broken off and prosperity will begin to return to your generations. *Grasping this concept and putting it into practice will literally change your family tree!*

The principle of blessing is found throughout the Bible. Men, I am so deeply convinced that adapting a Kingdom lifestyle that causes us to constantly speak a Father's Blessing over our families is crucial to rebuilding our homes and our country's culture. To firmly establish this understanding in our minds, we need to take a look at some of the Biblical texts that establish this most important Kingdom practice.

> *Then God blessed them, and God said to them, "Be fruitful and multiply; fill the earth and subdue it; have dominion over the fish of the sea, over the birds of the air, and over every living thing that moves on the earth."*

Genesis 1:28

Yahweh spoke this blessing over the first of His children, Adam and Eve. Talk about identifying and empowering them to fulfill a divine destiny – wow! Our Creator sets for us a tremendous example of how to bless our own children. He also established that a blessing is spoken directly to the one being blessed. A Father's words of blessing need to be heard by his children.

> *Then Isaac trembled exceedingly, and said, "Who? Where is the one who hunted game and brought it to me? I ate all of it before you came, and I have blessed him – and indeed he shall be blessed."*

Genesis 27:33

Isaac understood that a Father's Blessing cannot be taken away. Such a blessing is to be understood as permanent. This is why Paul wrote in Romans 11:29, *"the gifts and the calling of God are irrevocable."*

> *Then Israel (Jacob) saw Joseph's sons, and said, "Who are these?" And Joseph said to his father, "They are my sons, whom God has given me in this place." And he said, "Please bring them to me and I will bless them."*
> *So Joseph brought them from beside his knees, and he bowed down with his face to the earth. And he blessed Joseph. So he blessed them (Joseph's sons) that day, saying "By you Israel will bless, saying, "May God make you as Ephraim and as Manasseh!"*

Genesis 48:8-20

Jacob establishes a blessing still spoken over the sons of each Hebrew household every Erev Shabbat (evening of the Sabbath) to this day. "May God make you like Ephraim and Manasseh" is prayed over every male child in a Jewish family each Shabbat. For girls, it is Rachel and Leah, mothers of a great nation of Yahweh's children. Jacob laid his hands on each of the boys' heads, also establishing how Jewish fathers still bless their children.

The descendants of Ephraim and Manasseh would one day inherit some of the best land in the nation of Israel. "Ephraim" is the name applied to the Hebrews scattered among the nations to this very day and many of these are among the most prosperous people in the world. A good number of them are considered among the Lost Ten Tribes of Israel. (Many around the world, possibly even you, have no idea that they are literally of this "lost lineage".)

And God spoke to Moses, saying: "Speak to Aaron and his
sons, saying, 'This is the way you should bless the children of
Israel'. Say to them: 'Adonai will bless you and keep you;
Adonai will make his face shine upon you, and show you his
favor; Adonai will lift up his face toward you and give you
his peace.' In this way they are to put My name on the people
of Israel, so that I will bless them."

Numbers 6:22-27

This is astounding to me! Yahweh gives instruction to Aaron and his descendants (the priests of Israel) to speak His "Father's Blessing" over the children of Israel forever. To do this puts His name, His mark on us. We are set apart to be His children. We belong to Him and He will continue to empower us to prosper forever. He commands His priests to give His Father's Blessing to His children as often as possible. As the apostle Paul teaches, because of our redemption in Yeshua the Messiah, we are also priests in His kingdom. Men, need to bless one another and our families with these same words as often as possible.

Now the days of David drew near that he should die, and he
charged Solomon his son, saying "I go the way of all the
earth; be strong, therefore, and prove yourself a man. And
keep the charge of the LORD your God;
to walk in His ways, to keep His statues,

His commandments, His judgments, and
His testimonies, as it is written in the Law of Moses,
that you may prosper in all that you do."

I Kings 2:1-3

David, a man after Yahweh's own heart, continued the principle of blessing the sons of Israel by blessing Solomon with these instructive and powerful words. Solomon must have followed his father's instruction, for we all know that he became the wisest and richest man on earth. A Father's Blessing empowers our children to prosper!

...it came to pass that Jesus also was baptized; and while He
prayed, the heaven was opened. And the Holy Spirit
descended in bodily form like a dove upon Him, and a voice
came from Heaven which said, "You are My Beloved Son; in
You I am well pleased."

Luke 3:21-22

As Joseph of Nazareth was not Yeshua's biological father, he could not have given Yeshua the deepness of a true Father's Blessing. In Jewish culture Yeshua was considered a "mamzer", one of questionable birth. Though Yeshua most definitely experienced a Bar Mitzvah at age 13, the blessing of Joseph was not the blessing of His true Father. It is no little matter that His ministry was not released until He had heard from His true Father, *"You are my beloved Son; in You I am well pleased."* Yeshua, too, needed His Father's Blessing before He proceed into the most significant and powerful years of His life on earth.

And He (Yeshua) took them (the children) up in His arms,
put His hands on them, and blessed them.

Mark 10:16

Yeshua did not hesitate to speak a blessing over the children that had
gathered around him. The blessing He most likely spoke was the
very one established by Jacob: *"May God make you as Ephraim and*
as Manasseh!" To the girls, *"May God make you as Rachel and*
Leah!" as it was through them that Yahweh brought forth the lineage
of Israel, His nation of priests and kings. Perhaps Yeshua also spoke
over them the priest's blessing given to Aaron to speak over all those
of Israel. He most certainly would follow the pattern that He, as one
with the Father, gave to their forefathers.

By faith Isaac blessed Jacob and Esau concerning things to
come. By faith Jacob, when he was dying, blessed both the
sons of Joseph.

Hebrews 11:20-21

By faith, these men blessed their sons and grandsons. Is it possible
that blessing our children is an act of faith? Yes, it is. They desired a
prosperous, good life for their descendants. The forefathers of our
"faith" knew that the Father's Blessing was crucial to the future of
their families. Somehow we have completely lost this instruction and
understanding. Men, we have the opportunity to restore what has
been lost.

Finally, all of you be of one mind, having compassion for one another; love as brothers, be tenderhearted, be courteous; not returning evil for evil or reviling for reviling, but on the contrary blessing, knowing that you were called to this, that you may inherit a blessing.

I Peter 3:8-9

We are called to a lifestyle that blesses one another so that we will inherit the blessing of Yahweh! Tell me, gentlemen, how much blessing goes on in your home? In your church? Do you bless others in your workplace? Or do you curse them? Most of us have never had a Godly example of being men from whom blessings are the normal part of everyday conversations. I think it's time to change that, don't you?

Understanding the Significance of a Father's Blessing

In our culture today it is quite obvious that marriages are under serious attack. In the church, we understand that our enemy, Lucifer is out to break up homes and destroy Yahweh's ideal design for marriage and family life. Yet I believe our enemy is after much more than this. When there is no father in the home or a father that is ignorant of his role as the source of a Father's Blessing, the enemy knows that he is now capable of stopping a powerful impartation. Satan knows that this void will go far in instigating the destruction of the identity and destiny of the children in that home. When he succeeds at this effort in a family, he knows he has inflicted a void that will go on from generation to generation. That is, until someone who knows better rises up in that family and breaks off what has been done. That "someone" is now you!

Men, a father cannot release to his son what he does not know for himself. Thus a man void of his own manhood cannot pass that manhood on to his son, or exemplify a Godly husband and father to his daughter. Lucifer is not only after destroying your home. He is after destroying the generations your home will produce: your grandchildren and great grandchildren and beyond. **Men, you also need to know that your wife, whether your marriage is intact or not, cannot release a Father's Blessing into your children.** It is not her role, nor is it her responsibility. It is solely yours. Do not rob your children of your personal and unique blessing. I cannot emphasize this strongly enough!

You might be questioning just how the role of a father and mother differ in parenting. Though we will go into that more deeply later, I want to address that just a bit right now. Let's face it, in our modern church culture it is the women, the moms, that take care of almost all of child's upbringing. This is all the more so true in divorce situations. Guys, pay attention! Biblically, you are not allowed to be an absentee father at any level or circumstance. Why? The difference in your roles as mom and dad is as obvious as how a child is held in the arms of parents. Grab this understanding and your role as a father will quickly become clearly defined.

When a mother, the nurturer, holds an infant she usually holds the child face to face. The child can readily look into her eyes at any moment or nuzzle into her shoulder. Mom will speak comfort and encouragement to that little one. Women are designed by Yahweh to nurture our children and instruct them on how to nurture others. Mom will comfort, encourage and provide a place of security and refuge for your children. She will teach them how to be aware of the needs of others and meet them. Because of her unique role, both her sons and daughters will learn how to build and nurture their own future relationships by following her instructions and example.

However, when a father holds an infant he usually holds the child's back against his chest so baby is facing outward. The child's legs dangling freely below while he or she has full view of everything ahead. Papa is literally turning the child to face the world, which holds that child's future. Dad, your role is to prepare your child for adulthood. You are to impart identity and release blessing (empowerment) and destiny. You are to make sure your children have all the confidence, self–esteem, skills and Godly principles they will need to prosper and succeed in a world determined to ignore Yahweh and do things its own way. You play a key role in your child's ability to become who Yahweh has destined them to be and to accomplish. This is why understanding how to impart a Father's Blessing is so very crucial!

In the Hebrew culture, these differing but very important roles are practically applied in how a child is raised. Until a child reaches their Bar or Bat Mitzvah on their 13th birthday, Mom is primarily responsible for the everyday life of the child, nurturing and gently but firmly guiding the child by what she sees in them. Dad is very much involved in observing and encouraging the child's personality, interests, and abilities, but it is mom that is protecting and caring for them as only a mother can. At age 13, however, Dad becomes the one who takes the child under wing, especially his sons, seeing to their vocational and life skills training as well as modeling a healthy marriage relationship and good fatherhood. Dads have the ability to let a child try to fly on his or her own much more so than mom does. Dads can emotionally handle their crash landings a lot better. That is because Dad is nurturing a whole different set of skills that will empower them to survive the challenges of life outside the home.

This is exactly why in most divorced families, the children, at age 12 or 13 begin to gravitate toward their father. This may even be to the point of wanting to go live with Dad rather than stay with Mom. A child by God-given instinct knows that they need dad at this point in their life. They also internally know they need their Father's Blessing. They most likely will not be able to verbally express these needs to you. They can't explain it, but the yearning is there in their gut nonetheless. Weigh this out carefully, single parents. Husband

and wife may no longer need or want each other, but children will always need their parents to fulfill their ordained role in their lives. Make your choices wisely and responsibly as to how you will meet these needs in the lives of your children. This will affect your all of your future generations, so it is no light matter.

Men, though this is true for both dads and moms, I am speaking to you right now. You must grasp with certainty that you have a huge effect on the destiny of your children. Even if they are grown children, your input and your blessings in their lives is and always will always be critical. Especially that formal Father's Blessing that will propel them into adulthood – even if they are already 40 years old!

If you are still in need of receiving a Father's Blessing, I strongly encourage you to approach your father and ask him to bless you. If your father is no longer living, ask one who is a close father-figure to you to bless you. Your children, your father or your father-figure may not fully understand why this is so important to you. Don't be overly concerned about that. Experience has shown me that somewhere in the midst of actually doing this, a light comes on in their minds and hearts. Some will grasp it completely. For others, it will be just enough for them to at least personally value and treasure this time.

I also want to encourage those of you with children still at home. Speak a blessing over them, as often as possible, preferably every morning before your split up for the day. If your children are grown and out of the house, give them a phone call at least once a week and bless them. Trust me, it will mean the world to them. Those of you who are blessed to be "Grandpa", bless those grandkids, too. You will become even more endeared to them.

If you are pastor, may I address you pastor to pastor for a moment? (The rest of you men, please keep reading along simply because you need to understand this also.) I want to strongly encourage you to undertake providing a "blessing service" for the people of your congregations. In our congregation, we pattern ours after the Bar and Bat Mitzvahs of Jewish tradition. We are a Hebrew Roots congregation, so we have no problem calling them by their Hebrew titles. I cannot possibly overstress how important this ceremony is in the Body of Messiah. This Biblical rite of passage patterned after our Creators's own example of a Father's Blessing cannot be replaced by church confirmations or any other religious experience. The blessing of our children needs to come through their fathers. There is nothing in the world that can replace this.

Pastors, let me be direct with you as a leader and trainer of leaders. The men in your congregation who were never blessed and validated by their fathers desperately need to receive a Father's Blessing. (The women do also, but that's another full topic for another time.) You will release them into their potential as leaders in your congregation in a manner that no other event possibly can. This ceremony can be done for men of any age. Preparation can be crafted to meet specific seasons in man's life. In our congregation, we Bar Mitzvah men well into adulthood after they complete the Called to be Men program. I am always amazed at the profound affect it has on their ability to mature as believers, husbands and fathers. Our "graduates" become engaged in our congregation and actually look for service and leadership opportunities. In fact, we usually have more men than women attending our services on a regular basis. How many churches can claim that?!

What more can I say on this matter? The absence of a Father's Blessing is doing serious damage to the identity of men in our culture. A young man needs to be affirmed that he is a man with a very important role to fulfill in his household and community. He has been designed by Yahweh to fulfill that role and he needs to know that. When this is formally passed on to him in a positive framework, the challenge of manhood will inspire him. Older men, we also need to be blessed by our fathers or a prominent father figure in our lives. Far too many of us are still longing to be validated by our fathers. The biblical pattern of a Father's Blessing solves the issues of validation for young and old, generation by generation. Fathers, we need to actively bless our own sons. We need to take charge of establishing manhood in our sons and in the fatherless young men in our congregations. There is far too much at stake to be leaving this to chance.

For some reason known only to our Creator, without receiving a Father's Blessing, most men literally get stuck in an immature mindset and become stunted emotionally. Such a man trying to make his way through life will struggle to validate his own identity and attempt to release himself into adulthood in a variety of ways: drinking with the boys, joining fraternities and clubs to "belong" to something manly and greater than themselves, sexual conquests of women, pornography, joining a gang, entering the military merely to prove manhood, and becoming "married" to work and financial success. All of these are not the actions of a real man, but of a little boy trapped in a man's body no matter what his age.

Young girls need blessing and validation from their fathers so that they too can fully enter into womanhood. In an attempt to find validity and identity, they too are open to falling into the same "validity traps" as the boys. An invalidated woman, she will subconsciously try to gain that missing Father's Blessing from a boyfriend or husband. This is a huge danger that sets her up for possible abusive relationships. A young woman who has not been given a sense of great worth and a deep awareness of her father's love for her will seek these from another strong male figure. Her sense of identity, rather than deeply instilled within her by her father, will become dependent on what others think of her, especially men. In a worst case scenario, a woman's lack of validity and strong sense of worth sets her up for believing she actually deserves the poor or dangerous relationship she finds herself in. Fathers, your blessing and validation to your daughter may well save her from a horrible future relationship. Yes, a Father's Blessing is that important.

Think about this, fathers. When a young man and a young woman, both without validation and identity from a Father's Blessing, enter into a marriage, what is their potential for a truly marvelous, life-long relationship? Could it be that they will spend their entire married life together seeking for the other to give them the validation they are missing? Most likely. Sadly, the result will be disappointment, blame, anger and bitterness. They cannot receive something from their spouse that a spouse is unable to give. Yet they have no idea what is truly missing. The lack of a Father's Blessing might well have set your child up for a failed marriage, even a series of failed relationships as he or she spends a lifetime seeking for something only a father has the ability to provide. Yes, a Father's Blessing is that important.

The men in our communities and churches need to be validated and released. The leaders of our communities, schools, and churches need to grasp this concept and apply it. Our fathers need to be taught how to pick up this gift of blessing their children and run with it. The very lives of our children are at stake.

Preparing Your Child for a "Father's Blessing Ceremony"

A "Father's Blessing Ceremony" is a big celebration. It is the most important birthday party your child will ever have! Traditionally, a great deal of time and effort go into preparing for the event and we will get to those details later. Far more important than the party planning is the preparation of the child. Don't thrust this event on a child who has not been prepared for young adulthood. If you determine that they are not quite ready for this life status change, wait. It is not fair to the child to launch them into a new role in life just to make you look or feel good. Be wise. Be sure your child is ready. Some of you have a few years to wait before your children reach this 12- 13 year age range. You have time to prepare them. If your child is already in that range and you've done little to nothing to prepare them as needed, don't get ahead of things. Take the time needed to re-establish your fatherly role in their lives and work towards this day as your joint goal.

In either scenario, your children need to be involved and excited about this process. Each of your children should be looking forward to this event with great anticipation! For your son, this will be the day he becomes a man. For your daughter, this will be the day she becomes a woman. This will be one of the most significant days in his or her life. Be sure they are ready for it.

In the months and weeks before the ceremony, your son or daughter needs to be instructed in the changes that are about to take place in their life. Men, this is primarily your responsibility. Don't slough this off to your wife. She can be involved, but it is your responsibility to be fully engaged in ushering your child into adulthood, not hers.

Let's consider the important aspects of adult life that you will want to discuss with and instruct your child in before their special day. If you identify some areas in which you see they are struggling or have lots of questions, now is the time to help them. You are being given a tremendous opportunity to guide them away from what could be harmful or even tragic choices. In essence, you will be working with your child to create a lifestyle that they will walk out, and in which you will be in a fully supportive role, for the next five years.

»Physical and Emotional Changes

Your child will soon be undergoing the physical and emotional changes of puberty and young adulthood. These changes may already be underway. There will be dating relationships ahead. We want our sons and daughters to move into this time in their life with correct and Godly understanding. Be sure that your son or daughter knows the truth about romance, love, marriage and sex at this crucial time of releasing them into adulthood.

Fathers should discuss with their sons the role of being a man. Our boys need to know the difference between lust and healthy attraction. They need to know how to handle their thought life concerning girls. They also need to be instructed on how to treat a woman with honor, respect and dignity – no matter their age. Your son needs to know that one day it will be his responsibility to provide for and protect a family of his own. That responsibility begins with his relationship to the woman he marries. He needs to know that dating is serious business.

As he begins to interact with girls of his own age, he needs to give serious thought to the qualities and faith walk that he will one day want in a wife and determine to not become involved with any girl who isn't pursuing these in her life. He should also give serious thought to how he will become the type of young man such a wonderful young woman would want to spend her life with. Also make it clear to him that Yahweh's best for his life is that he remains sexually pure until he marries. Make sure he knows that he can trust you to help him remain so. He needs to know he can easily and openly bring his questions, struggles and concerns in this area to you.

Fathers should discuss with their daughter the role of being a woman, even if it may be embarrassing. She needs to be confident that you as her father recognize that she is no longer a child and has her own unique identity. The gifts, skills, interests and positive character attributes she possesses need to be validated and encouraged by you. In fact, she needs to be made so confident in her unique and positive identity that she will not allow her identity to be twisted or changed by anyone she dates, or her future spouse.

She also needs to be given your protocol for dating. If you don't have one, Dad, you need to create one. She needs to know that you are going to be watching over her, not to control her, but to protect her. Help her understand that dating, though fun, is also serious business. Dating's primary function is to find that future spouse. It leaves a person wide open emotionally and physically. Without guidelines, yours and hers, dating can lead to some unnecessary painful experiences. Help your daughter set her own guidelines and understand why your guidelines for her are what they are.

Encourage your daughter to give serious thought to what kind of young man she would really want to walk through life with. What would be his character and attributes? What does his faith walk need to be? Help her grasp how important it is that she not waste her time on any young man that isn't already pursuing that character and lifestyle. Encourage her in the wisdom of protecting her heart.

Also make it clear that Yahweh's best for her is that she remains sexually pure until she marries. She needs to know that she has the right and privilege to guard her purity. She needs to know she has the right to resist and cut off any influence or relationship that would try to convince her otherwise. Your empowerment and your commitment to protect her at her request in this area of her life will be priceless to her.

»*Adult Responsibilities*

Your son or daughter needs to understand that after their special day of blessing there will be a change in the level and content of responsibilities in their life. More will be expected of them in the home, in the family business, in the congregation and in other areas of life you as parents deem important to their development. In our society, your child now has a mere five years to learn a great deal about their roles in each of those areas. There are life skills that they need to acquire and our school system does not adequately train them in these skills. Do they know how to cook, clean, balance a check book, create and follow a budget, save and invest, handle credit, fill out a financial statement, get a car repaired, apply for a job, or even start a business if they so desire? Equip them! (If you cannot prepare them to handle finances, I highly recommend Dave Ramsey's course for teens. You can learn right alongside them!)

»Occupational Choices

This age of 12 to 13 is a crucial time for parents to firmly plant the seed that, as heirs in Yahweh's Kingdom, your child has been created to be the head, not the tail; above and not beneath. Encourage your child to set his or her sights high. Help them identify their passions, interests, and talents. Then encourage them to search out vocations in which they can be leaders and innovators. Encourage them to consider becoming business people, making them the employers rather than the employed. Above all else, instill in them that they never have to "settle for less" when it comes to their life's calling. Prepare them for times of struggle and failure, but instill in them that it is never okay to give up. Help your child nurture a deep sense of God-given destiny. Teach them the concept of having a life-mission statement and help them begin to create one. They most likely won't have a clue as to the details, but at this age they should be able to grasp a sense of direction and purpose. Help them find resources that will give them opportunities and tools to build toward that future career of interest to them. Stir up their passion to succeed. Don't be discouraged if they change their minds. Give them the opportunity to explore their own career potential *now*.

»Spiritual Responsibility

Hopefully by this point in life, your child has been taught the ways of Yahweh as found in the Bible, beginning in Genesis. If you see areas of lack of training, this is the time to determine how to help them get the knowledge and understanding that they still need. It is also crucial for them to understand that they are now going to be responsible for their personal spiritual growth. No longer can they lean on the faith of their parents. Your child's faith needs to become their own. His or her relationship with Yeshua HaMashiach (the Messiah) is now completely in their hands.

As a pastor, it grieves me to say that many churches are often lacking in good Biblical instruction. Encourage your child to always be a student of the Word of Yahweh and pursue His Truth in all things. Encourage them to become active and involved in your congregation. (Remember, they learn best through example. Are *you* active and involved in your congregation?) Help them learn how to measure their own spiritual progress and take responsibility for that. Do they understand how to read and study Yahweh's Word for themselves? Have they grasped and applied key eternal truths like salvation, living a set apart life, confession, repentance and applying the wisdom of the Bible practically in their lives? Is their faith evident in how they are responding to Father Yahweh and interacting with others? Dad, be proactive and create a plan with your child on how they can become as fully spiritually equipped as possible for adulthood by the day they graduate high school.

The Day the Rubber Hits the Road

Above all else, remember that the lifestyle that you as a parent present for them to walk out during their young adult, high school years should both challenge and excite them. You have the opportunity to be the most important role model and mentor in their life. This special ceremony that you are creating for them is the launching pad that will propel them into their future. Do your best to make it a good launch toward positive results. Let your child know that you are there to guide and instruct them and that you will continue to always guard their safety. Let them also know that you remain their parent and always will be. You want their life to be long and prosperous, therefore you still expect be honored and obeyed!

Planning a "Father's Blessing Ceremony"

Please understand that this is not an event to be taken lightly or planned at the last minute. In Jewish culture, this event (called a Bar Mitzvah for boys and a Bat Mitzvah for girls) often has the same energy and finances spent on it as the child's wedding will one day incur. That is certainly not a requirement, but it does indicate the understood weight of this ancient ceremony. The ceremony is to be orchestrated by the father, though both parents oversee the full event. The day usually entails inviting guests to witness this rite of passage and celebrate with you. A special meal or refreshments are usually served. Some families hire a caterer and band of musicians or a DJ for dancing and ambiance. Some provide a big barbeque. Others keep it all a little lower key. It is really up to your family's preferences. If you would like to pattern the day's celebration after the more traditional Hebrew event, you will want to do some research and possibly consult a Messianic pastor for input and guidance. If such a minister is available in your community, he or she might also be available to conduct the ceremony, working with you in the planning and arrangements.

At one point in the ceremony, your child should be expected to read aloud or quote from memory a portion of Scripture. (See the "Sample Ceremony" later in this chapter.) They should start memorizing the passage or practice their reading of it aloud weeks before the ceremony. Encourage them to be prepared, as "being diligent in preparation" is a desirable adult attribute! During the ceremony, there will be powerful moments that your child will never forget for the rest of his or her life. The sound of your voice and the words you say to them in this public event will be replayed in their memory often and forever.

Don't be too laid back in this, men. **You need to be prepared!** This day is far too important to be lax with. Invest prayer and careful thought to each word and action you plan for that day. If you are not good with "this kind of stuff", ask someone you trust and who knows your child to help you craft your words and the ceremony. You don't have to speak from memory, so write your thoughts and blessing down and simply read it out loud. If you are not comfortable leading the ceremony yourself, ask your pastor or a family member, even a good friend, to be your "master of ceremonies". Remember, this day is about celebrating the adult your child is becoming. Make it a great one!

A Sample Ceremony

Here are a few suggestions. If you have prepared your child as above, they will not be taken off guard by any it.

1. Welcome your guests and open with a prayer. Perhaps sing a song of worship together.

2. Provide your guests with a brief explanation of what this event is about and how important it is in the life of your child. Consider using I Corinthians 13:11 in your opening remarks. "When I was a child, I spoke as a child, I understood as a child, I thought as a child; but when I became a man, I put away childish things." (Remember, Paul was a Jew. He passed through this ceremony himself at age 13. It was the day that he "became a man".)

3. Call your son or daughter forward and speak to them some instruction as they move forward into adulthood.

4. Assure your child that Yahweh has a purpose and destiny for them.

   I know the thoughts that I think toward you, says the LORD, thoughts of peace and not evil, to give you a future and a hope. **Jeremiah 29:11**

And we know that all things work together for good to those who love God, to those who are the called according to His purpose. For whom He foreknew He also predestined to be conformed to the image of His Son, that He might be the firstborn among many brethren. Moreover whom He predestined, these He also called, these He also justified; and whom He justified, these He also glorified. **Romans 8:28-30**

5. Validate your child's unique identity. State the talents, gifts, and skills that you see in them and commend them for these.

6. Recognize your child's spiritual growth and their relationship with Yeshua as being the foundation of their life today and throughout their adulthood. This is the most significant point to today's celebration. Publicly charge your child that from this day forward, they will be responsible for their spiritual growth and that you are there to guide them in that pursuit. Encourage them that keeping their relationship with Yeshua strong and vibrant is the most crucial aspect of their adult life. Encourage them to study the Word of God and allow the Holy Spirit to teach and guide them with it. Encourage them that by living out God's instructions and principles found in the Bible from a heart of love for the Messiah is true faith and that walking this path will bring to him/her a fulfilling and blessed life that will allow them to be a source of blessing to their family, congregation, and community.

7. Announce to your guests that today your child is entering adulthood and is beginning the important journey of taking on the life and responsibilities of an adult. Assure your child that you know that they will miss the mark from time to time, but that you are there for them and will do all that you can to help them discover how to succeed with their dreams and goals. Express your confidence in them as they pursue education and establishing a vocation.

8. Declare your anticipation over their eventual selection of a spouse and one day presenting you with grandchildren but let them know that they don't need to be in any rush on this! Publically encourage them be patient, setting their sights high and going for the best Yahweh has for them in this area of marriage and family. Express your confidence in them to make wise relationship choices and to stay sexually pure. (Yes, this will embarrass the daylights out them, but that's okay! They will never be able forget your instruction to them and your confidence in them.)

9. Encourage them to become involved in their community and congregation as a role model to their peers and the children following behind them. Encourage your child that as they become leaders they are to do so with a servant heart. Remind them that they are always to have a watchful eye out for those in need around them and help those who sincerely need help and encouragement.

10. Have your child read aloud a selected portion of Scripture. This is very important! A daughter might want to read Proverbs 31: 10-31. A son might want to read Proverbs 13. Other possibilities for either gender would be Deuteronomy 6:1-9 or 28:1-14.

11. The Father's Blessing. Father and child now stand face to face before the guests. Place your right hand on your child's head and speak (or read) your blessing over them. Below you will find a sample blessing that you can use as it is or adapt as you desire.

12. Present your child with a gift to mark this special occasion perhaps a ring or locket, a prayer shawl (Tallit), a plaque or certificate, a study Bible; something that recognizes the

significance of this moment of passage from childhood to adulthood.

13. Present your son or daughter to your gathered guests as Mr. or Miss! Your son or daughter should now take this opportunity to thank the guests for coming to witness and celebrate this very important day in his or her life. Then he or she should invite the guests to enjoy the refreshments and give them direction to that location.

14. Let the congratulations and the party begin!

An Example: Father's Blessing for Sons

Son (use the child's name), before Yahweh (God) and all these witnesses, as your father, I declare that today you are a man. By following the Torah (Word of God) and its Principles you have become equipped with everything you need to accomplish your destiny as a man of Yahweh (God). You are one who would walk in the Paths of Righteousness of our Messiah Yeshua. I today publically recognize what Yahweh has done inside of you.

I pray the Heavenly Father's Blessing over you. You are no longer a little boy. You are a man of Elohim (God), a man of virtue, a man of integrity, a man of wisdom and a man of honor. You were chosen and put here on the earth for a specific purpose. You were only in your mother's womb for nine months, but Yahweh carried you in His Spirit for thousands of years, before the foundations of the earth. You are called to be a man, to complete the destiny that Yahweh gave only to you.

I give you this instruction today, as David did to his son, Solomon. *"Be strong, therefore, and prove yourself a man. And keep the charge of Yahweh your Elohim; to walk in His ways, to keep His statures, His commandments, His judgments, and His testimonies, as it is written in the Law of Moses, that you may prosper in all that you do and wherever you turn."* (I Kings 2:2-3)

I also encourage you with the words of our Messiah Yeshua. *"If you love me, obey my commandments."* (John 14:15)

Today, hear your Heavenly Father say, "My son, I love you! I bless you and expect you to prosper in all you do. Because Messiah Yeshua lives in you, you are a direct seed, a descendant, of Abraham, Isaac, and Jacob. My covenant with them also belongs to you. You will be blessed when you go out and blessed when you go in."

Today you are loosed from being your Mom's little boy. I release you into the authority and responsibility of manhood. You have been given the gift of proclaiming "Behold the Lamb" to the Nations. You are an Ambassador, a Shaliach, of the Most High Elohim. You will reverence His Name, His Lifestyle and serve Him with all of your heart, mind, and soul. There is a gifting and anointing on your life. You are unique. There is no one like you!

Son, I choose to bless you with wisdom from Yahweh, an attitude of honor, sexual purity and marital fidelity. A man who lives in awe of Adonai will be praised. May your wife and your children for a thousand generations be blessed. May your acts of service, your business, your finances and all of your relationships be blessed and prosper.

Today I proclaim before Yahweh and all these witnesses: This is my son, in whom I am well pleased.

An Example: Father's Blessing for Daughters

Daughter (use the child's name), you have so many awesome characteristics and attributes that have been given to you by Yahweh (God). By following the Torah (Word of God) and its Principles you have become equipped with everything you need to accomplish your destiny as a woman of Yahweh (God). You are one who would walk in the Paths of Righteousness of our Messiah Yeshua (Jesus). Today I publically recognize what Yahweh has done inside of you.

In Jeremiah 1:5 Yahweh tells you, *"Before I formed you in the womb I knew you; before you were born I sanctified you; I ordained you a prophet to the nations."* Yahweh has carried you in His Spirit for thousands of years, even before the foundations of the earth were formed. You are a woman of Yahweh that has been prepared for these last days to be voice for Him. You are one that will carry His standard in your home, your community and wherever He might send you. You have been chosen since before time began to be His Bride. You were born for such a time as this.

Today you are loosed from being your Mom's little girl. I release you into the authority and the responsibility of womanhood. I pray that Yahweh will bless you as you walk out your unique destiny, given to you by the Most High Elohim. I pray that just as you have chosen to honor your parents He will bring you long life and prosperity. I pray that will give you good health all the days of your life.

Today, hear your Heavenly Father say, "My daughter, I love you! I bless you and expect you to prosper in all you do. Because Messiah Yeshua lives in you, you are a direct seed, a descendant, of Abraham, Isaac, and Jacob. My covenant with them also belongs to you. You will be blessed when you go out and blessed when you go in.

Daughter, I choose to bless you with wisdom from Yahweh, virtue, sexual purity, and marital fidelity. A woman who lives in awe of Adonai shall be praised. May your husband praise you for your diligence and your excellence in all that you put your hands to accomplish. May your children rise up and call you blessed. May your descendants for a thousand generations be blessed. May all of your relationships, your acts of service, your business, your finances, and your household be blessed and prosper.

Today I proclaim before Yahweh and all these witness: This is my beloved daughter, in whom I am well pleased!

Chapter Three:
Choosing A Lifestyle of Honor

...for those who honor Me I will honor,
and those who despise Me shall be lightly esteemed.

I Samuel 2:30

He who follows righteousness and mercy finds life,
righteousness and honor.

Proverbs 21:21

In Chapter One, I introduced honor as one of the foundational attributes of a Real Man. In this chapter, I want to help you understand honor on a very practical level. What does honor look like on a day to day basis? How does it play out in our homes, on the job and in our relationship with Yahweh? As I stated before, honor is so critically important to Yahweh, and yet it is so seriously lacking in our current culture, both outside and inside the church. I do not hesitate a moment, men, to proclaim that the essence of the Gospel message, from Genesis to Revelation, is "honor". Yeshua was and is the full and perfect example of a man of honor. In these Last Days before our King's return, we need to make every effort to restore honor in our homes, congregations and communities. As we do so, may we also see honor restored to the culture of our nation.

Because this is such a crucial matter, let's first refresh our memory on what honor is. **Honor is "esteem due or paid to worth; high estimation; respect; consideration; reverence; veneration; a manifestation of respect or reverence; a mark of respect; a**

ceremonial sign of consideration; to revere; to treat with deference and submission; when used of the Supreme Being, to reverence; to adore; to worship. To dignify; to raise to distinction or notice; to elevate in rank or station; to treat in a complimentary manner or with civility." In basic terms, "honor" means to give high esteem and high respect to others.

I now want to take you a little deeper into the meaning of honor – from a Hebrew perspective! **The Hebrew word translated as "honor" is "kabod"**; the same Hebrew word that is also translated as "glory". **The full meaning of "kabod" is to "make weighty: abounding with, boast, glorify, make glorious, glory, make heavy, lay heavily, honor, be honorable, noble, prevail, promote (to honor), be rich."** [Strong's #H3513]

If you've spent much time in charismatic or Pentecostal circles, folks are always talking about "the Glory of God" falling down on them. They are looking for this "glory" to be a manifest presence of Yahweh. Based on the Hebrew definition, the "Glory of God" isn't something that is going to fall or manifest simply because we pray, sing, speak in tongues and so forth. The glory, or honor, of Yahweh our Elohim (God) will "lay heavily" upon His people only when they are living an honorable, noble lifestyle 7 days a week according to His ways, not our own. This is the Kingdom reality that most Christians get hung up on. We want Yahweh's glory, honor and favor to rest on us. However, we like to set our own definition about what that looks like, rather than listening to and following the King's instructions on these matters.

The ancient Israelites understood this very well. From the days in the wilderness with Moses to the days of David's Tabernacle and Solomon's Temple, they as a nation or community had the manifest presence of Yahweh dwelling with them day by day as long as they followed His honorable and noble ways. They fully understood that listening and obeying was not a matter of salvation or atonement.

That was covered by the blood of sacrificed lambs and goats. However, keeping the everyday presence of Yahweh in their everyday human lives was a matter of hearing and obeying. When their day by day lifestyles, not just their lips, proclaimed the character of Elohim (God), He blessed them with His presence, His favor and His peace.

Think about this in terms of our own lives, men. To possess Biblical honor in our lives on a daily basis means living our lives as Yahweh directs. This brings honor to Him, nothing less. This allows Him, as King of the Universe, to bestow His honor upon us. To have the honor of the King of the Universe laying heavy on our lives, on our families and congregations! What an awesome and powerful reality that would be! This Kingdom principle is exactly what Moses declared over the people of Yahweh in Deuteronomy 28.

> *Now it shall come to pass, if you diligently obey the voice of the Yahweh your God, to observe carefully all His commandments which I command you today, that Yahweh your God will set you high above all the nations of the earth. And these blessings shall come upon you and overtake you, because you obey the voice of the Yahweh your God.* **Deuteronomy 28:1-2**

Yahweh has every desire and intent to let His kabod, His glory and honor, fully manifest in our lives. This will happen when we are diligent in living lives of honor and glory according to His ways, not our own. Again, this is not about trying to earn our deliverance or salvation. That is possible only by the atoning blood of the Perfect Lamb, Yeshua the Messiah. Once we pass through His blood and our sin (dishonor) is fully atoned (made right), we step into His Kingdom. Our salvation, gentlemen, is a matter of "stepping in". *Now that we've done that, we must learn how to live in His Kingdom.* This life-long learning process is called "redemption", or as the apostle Paul describes it: "the working out of your salvation".

Our world and our cultures have been broken for a long time. We have so much to learn from Him and put into daily practice.

Yahweh's Kingdom has a lifestyle, one that is full of ongoing mercy, compassion, grace, forgiveness, honor and glory. That lifestyle is set before us in the Torah – the Principles and Instructions of Yahweh. The Torah lifestyle was perfectly lived out by Yeshua as He walked on the earth 2000 years ago and it will continue to be walked out by Him when He returns. What once judged and condemned us before our acceptance of Him as our Lamb and our King, now becomes "the perfect law of liberty" (James 1:25), teaching us how to walk in the abundant life Yeshua spoke of; one that is overtaken by His blessings! The life of the Torah is not heavy and burdensome, because it is now written on our hearts and minds. The Spirit of Yahweh now dwells within us, ready to empower and cause us to become men of honor. All that is required is a choice and a commitment to action. The choice is to stop wandering around, uncertain and confused and start following the ways of our King. The action is to study, listen and do as He instructs. The prophet Jeremiah's words once again speak loudly to us.

> *Thus says the Yahweh: "Stand in the ways and see, and ask for the old paths, where the good way is, and walk in it; Then you will find rest for your souls."* **Jeremiah 6:16**

Let me ask you this, man to man: Who is Yeshua to you? Is the King of the Universe *your* King? Or is He just another religious figure – another god among the many gods of this world? Your answer to this question will be the biggest issue in your life in the days we are already entering in to. The lifestyle you give honor (weight) to, His or the world's (your own) reveals your choice. Action, my friend, will always speak louder than words.

Author Gary Smalley (family counselor, president and founder of the Smalley Relationship Center) writes, "Honor is a decision we make to place high value and importance on another person by viewing them as a priceless gift and granting them a position of high respect." I couldn't agree more. Honor is a decision...one that is made every day, in every circumstance and with every person we encounter.

To place a high value and importance on our spouse, children, parents, employer, employees, friends, extended family members, leaders, and even a complete stranger is done so by intention and effort. As a representative of Yahweh's Kingdom on earth, I do my best to sincerely treat others as a priceless gift in my life. I encourage the people in our congregation to do the same. Every person that walks into our lives is a gift and brings that gift to us. (This also means that I am a gift and should be giving of my gift to others!) I make every effort to give each person I interact with each day my high respect.

To be a man of capable of giving such honor requires honesty. Honesty means that we are truthful, trustworthy and genuine. Our "yes" means "yes" and our "no" means "no". We are men of our word. We keep the promises that we make. We show up on time for the events we commit ourselves to: work, meetings, church services, dates with our spouse and events with our children. When we promise to mow the folk's yard on Sunday afternoon or help a friend repair his roof, we do it. We fully engage in the present moment, not allowing ourselves to be distracted by other things or thoughts. Being "fully present" is important, guys, especially to our wives and children. Nothing can be more dishonoring or disrespectful than not hearing what they are saying to us in conversation, or constantly answering our cell phones when out on "date night" or playing with our kids in the backyard. Undivided attention is often the highest form of honor we can give to another person and something that is increasingly a challenge to do in our smart phone crazy world. You and I have the power to change that, if we choose to.

Gentlemen, I challenge you with this Real Man image to pursue: Our thoughts shall harbor no ill will toward others. Our words are always trustworthy. Our actions consistently reveal a heart of respect and goodwill to everyone. We make every effort to be genuine; "the real deal". As we walk in this manner, the integrity of Yahweh and His Word will be held high as light to the world. Our personal integrity will also open the door for us to receive honor, favor and blessings, both from Yahweh and from man.

> *YHVH (Yahweh), who can rest in your tent [tabernacle]? Who can live on your holy mountain? Those who live a blameless life, who behave uprightly, who speak truth from their hearts and keep their tongues from slander; who never do harm to others or seek to discredit neighbors; who look with scorn on the vile, but honor those who fear YHVH; who hold to an oath, no matter the cost; who refuse usury when they lend money and refuse a bribe to damage the innocent. Those who do these things never will be moved.* **Psalm 15:1-5**

The Hebrew people have long understood the role of honor in achieving a successful life. They are of the whole House of Israel, the nation made up of the twelve tribes of Israel (Jacob), the descendants of Abraham and Isaac. Yahweh called them out from among all the nations of the earth to deliver them from its fallen world systems and re-establish His Kingdom ways upon the earth. Destined to be His light and carry His presence to the nations, they learned (often by trial and error) the soundness and integrity of Yahweh's Word. In simple terms, "it is so because Yahweh said so!"

Jews and Hebrew-roots Christians make it an everyday practice to speak aloud Deuteronomy 6:4-5 in their daily prayers. In fact, the verses themselves have become a prayer to them.

> *She'ma, Y'isreal! ADONAI Eloheinu, ADONAI echad, [Hear, Israel! YHVH our God, YHVH is one]; and you are to love*

ADONAI your God with all your heart, all your being and all your resources. **Deuteronomy 6:4-5**

These are the same verses Yeshua spoke in Matthew 22, Mark 12 and Luke 10 in response to the challenge of the Pharisee who asked which is the greatest commandment. To the Hebrew ear, the word "she'ma" means much more than "hear". It means "listen and obey". We are to do so out of a heart of love, giving everything of ourselves to Him. This is the greatest honor a man can give to Yahweh.

From this foundational of all honors, the Hebrew people are taught by Yahweh to also honor each other and to seek wisdom. They also understand the crucial difference between wisdom and honor. Wisdom does not prosper you financially. Wisdom teaches. With wisdom you know right from wrong, good from evil, clean from unclean and reward versus punishment. Honor, however, does prosper you! Honor will take you further than your intelligence, your education and your imagination. Honor qualifies you for promotion and advancement. Wisdom might grant you access to prosperity, but advancing into prosperity comes to you by your ability to give honor.

There are three levels of honor in our lives. 1) Those above us. 2) Those at our own level. 3) Those we serve or have under our care. Listening, obeying an instruction, willingness to change, respecting authority, holding a person in high esteem, being genuinely gracious and grateful in your attitude no matter what the circumstances, speaking positively to and about the people in your life, helping others, keeping your word – all of this speaks to a man who knows how to place high value on the lives of others. Honor has nothing to do with education, IQ or our dreams. Yet it has everything to do with achieving our dreams. What do you dream about? A good home with a wonderful wife and children? Having a great job? Owning your own successful business? Leading a healthy, vibrant ministry? The ability to honor others is your key to success in all of these areas.

Prosperity comes to those who have passed the test in honoring others. I can speak with the authority that comes from personal experience. Dishonoring someone in your life will lead to poverty and heartache. I have been there and done that; not going there again. I have seen far too many others walk down that same unhappy path. Men, if you lack finances, if you are suffering from damaged marriages and rocky relationships with children and other family members, there is good news. You have the ability to turn it all around. Find out who you have dishonored and ask for forgiveness. Then begin to honor them.

I have found that the biggest obstacle in my ability to honor others is my own attitude. When I allow myself to sink into a lack of gratitude and thankfulness, I stop honoring the people around me. Each morning I have to put on my "Attitude of Gratitude". I have to commit myself to walking in this attitude, first toward Yahweh and my family, and then toward all others I will encounter that day.

Practical Ways to Give Honor

Because honor is so pivotal in our growth and success in life, I want to provide you with some practical ideas that will help you put your attitude of gratitude into action right away. These actions are not hard, guys. They begin with a decision on your part to engage yourself in a lifestyle of honor by choosing to express your gratefulness to Yahweh and all those around you for who they are and their role in your life. I trust that my simple suggestions will prime the pump, so to speak, in your ability to come up with all sorts of ways you can honor others.

»*Honoring Yahweh*

Honoring Yahweh begins with a conscious every day decision to *she'ma*, listen and obey. Our obedience, out of a heart's response of love and gratitude, honors him as our Father and as our King.

There are two aspects to daily obedience. First, there are the written instructions and principles He has already provided for us in His Word, Genesis through Revelation. Second, as His sons, we all receive directives by the Holy Spirit each day in the paths and actions that are best for us. "Turn right, not left." "Give this man $10.00." "Go back to college and finish your degree." "You need to call your mom today." She'ma! Listen and obey!

- **Prayer honors Yahweh**. Talking with Him opens your life to Him, allowing Him to have access in areas that need His divine intervention. Men, you are His grown children – not infants. As your Father (and by the terms of His own covenant) He will not access any area in your life unless He is invited to do so. Seeking out your Abba (father) for his insight, instruction and guidance tells Him that you trust Him. Worshipping with words of gratitude and praise tells him that you have a healthy awe of Him (known as the "fear of the Lord"). A prayerless life, men, is a life that dishonors Yahweh.

- **Bring the King your tithes and offerings**. This honors Yahweh. Abraham understood that after gaining the spoils of war and reaping the prosperity that came from the keeping the principles of his covenant with Yahweh, he owed Yahweh his honor. He gave a tenth of his gain to Melchizedek, the priest of the Most High God not to appease Yahweh, but to properly honor Him. (Genesis 14:10-20) The tithe, the offerings and the first fruits of our seasonal harvests all belong to Yahweh. To hold them back for "me" dishonors Yahweh by robbing Him of what is His to begin with. He cannot honor those who dishonor Him. In fact, such dishonor brings death to the fruitfulness of our lives.

"Can a person rob God? Yet you rob me. But you ask 'How have we robbed you?' In tenths [tithes] and voluntary contributions [offerings]. A curse is on you, on your whole nation, because you rob me. Bring the whole tenth into the storehouse, so there will

be food in my house, and put me to the test," says Yahweh Tzva'ot [LORD of Heaven's Armies]. "See if I won't open for you the floodgates of heaven and pour out a blessing far beyond your needs. For your sakes I will forbid the devourer to destroy the yield from your soil; and your vine will not lose its fruit before harvest time," says Yahweh Tzva'ot. "All the nations will call you happy, for you will be a land of delights." **Malachi 3:7-12**

Are you struggling to make ends meet each month? I have to be blunt, gentlemen. Let me ask you, "Are you tithing and bringing Yahweh your offerings?" If you are dishonoring the King by robbing Him in tithes and offerings, he is even further robbed of the opportunity to bless you. You rob Yahweh *twice*. In doing so, you bring lack upon yourself and your household. Choose to honor Him and He will pour out a blessing far beyond your needs. He is the King. You have His Word on it.

- **Keeping the Sabbath honors Yahweh**. The Hebrew word is Shabbat and interestingly there is only one day of the week that is literally named Shabbat. We call it Saturday (named after a pagan god, as are all the days of the week on our Greek/Roman calendar). The Hebrew number the days; the days have no names. Only the seventh day has a name, a function. That day is called Shabbat.

The Sunday "Lord's Day" most Christians observe was not a Christian day of rest until 300 years after the death and resurrection of Yeshua. Men, Sunday is not the Biblical Shabbat established by the very words of Yahweh. Sunday is "the Lord's Day" by the edict of a Roman Emperor who had no love for the Hebrew God or His people. It took Rome 1200 years to get a majority of Christians to stop observing the Biblical Shabbat. (Don't believe me? Do the research. It is appalling.) She'ma! Listen and obey! This is what honors Him. Keep His Shabbat. He made it for you.

Thus the heavens and the earth were finished, along with everything in them. On the seventh day God was finished with his work which he had made, so he rested on the seventh day from all of his work which he had made. God blessed the seventh day and separated it as holy [not common]; because on that day God rested from all his work which he had created, so that it itself could produce. **Genesis 2:1-3**

I have news for you, men. Shabbat is not a Jewish thing. Shabbat is a Kingdom of God thing. The first Shabbat shared by YHVH with Adam and Eve was 2300 years before the first Hebrew, Abraham, walked upon the earth. Shabbat is a Bride and Groom thing. This is a day of celebration, delight, and intimacy between Yeshua, our Groom, and us, His Bride. In fact, Shabbat is our wedding ring – the sign of our eternal covenant with Him. (Ezekiel 20:12) Come sunset Friday night He is looking for His Bride, the love of His life! It's "date night". How dishonored would you feel if your bride didn't show up for a date night with you? He feels the same way. He set the time and looks forward to it with great passion and expectation. He is the Lord of the Sabbath and he made this time just for you. (Mark 2:23-28) Do you show up or is he spending those 24 hours without you? Do you wear your "wedding ring" with pride and joy or have you, like the widow with the ten coins, lost this very precious treasure? (The ten coins represent the Ten Commandments.)

- **Honor Yahweh by honoring His Feasts**. Seriously, this should be so simple for us to comprehend! We claim to live in His Kingdom. We claim Him to be our King. Yet, when He appoints for us Royal Days of celebration and honoring Him with our presence, we His own children, don't show up. What would you do if you were the King in this scenario? Most Christians have no idea that there are seven Royal Feast Days each year in His Kingdom. The first four feasts take place in the spring. They are (by their English names) Passover, the Day of First Fruits, the

Feast of Unleavened Bread, and Pentecost. The Day of the Trumpet, the Day of Atonement and the Feast of Tabernacles take place in autumn. (See Leviticus 23 for Yahweh's concise listing and instructions on the feast days.)

Yahweh's entire redemptive plan for mankind and the earth are ordered according to these seven huge celebrations. Yeshua's first coming fulfilled the prophecies found in the first four feasts of spring. Yeshua's second coming will fulfill the prophecies found in the three fall feasts.

Men, it is time to wake up to historical truth. Easter and Christmas are fully rooted in the worship of pagan gods. Their spiritual roots and meanings are deeply embedded in the Kingdom of Darkness. To our great detriment we have lost knowledge of Yahweh's Kingdom celebrations, which belong solely to the Kingdom of Light. We have unwisely abandoned their observance. How can we understand the fullness of who Yeshua is, what he has done for us and what our future with him is going be like if we do not know the times and seasons of His Kingdom? It doesn't matter how we feel or think about these substitute "holy days" created by religious men. What matters is what YHVH our King feels and thinks about them. He is quite clear in His instruction. Have nothing to do with pagan gods and their ways, period. Rather, honor Him by celebrating the days of rejoicing that He *as our King* has established for us.

Read the four gospels, men, and take note. Yeshua honored the seventh day Shabbat and all of the appointed Feast Days of Yahweh as established by Him in the Torah. He honored the Father by honoring his Word. Yeshua expects his followers to honor Him by living as He did and doing the same.

»Honoring Your Parents

Honoring parents can be a real challenge for some. Not all of us have a healthy relationship with one or both of our parents. The hard truth is that our parents are not perfect people. For some men, honoring a parent has to begin with forgiving them. That doesn't mean that you allow a parent to keep harming you. However, it does mean that you forgive them for their harm and dry up that root of bitterness that can take hold in you. A root of bitterness will eventually destroy you in one or more areas of your own life. Forgiveness is the only remedy.

I encourage those of you who have been deeply hurt by a parent to choose to forgive. They may never change. That doesn't matter. Your unforgiveness won't change them either. The only person unforgiveness hurts is you. Unforgiveness is a poison. To refuse to forgive is the same as drinking that poison and then expecting the other person to die. Forgive your parents, men. This is the first step to being able to give them honor.

What do we do if we are guilty of dishonoring our parents? I had to deal with that question in my own life. I grew up on a dairy farm and worked side by side with my dad before sunrise, after school, and well past sunset almost every day of my childhood and youth. I never had a summer off to have fun and goof around. As a teenager and young adult, I chose to rebel against my parents. In fact, I eventually became a biker and rebelled against life in general. I did and said a lot of things that deeply dishonored my parents and my family.

When I gave my life to Yeshua and entrusted Him to show me how to clean up my life and live according to His ways, my dishonor of my parents was one thing I knew I had to take care of. I owed them a deep, sincere apology and asked for their forgiveness. When I embraced the Hebrew roots of my faith over a decade ago, the Fifth Commandment to honor our parents became even more real to me. My dad had already passed away, but my mom was still with us. I purposed in my heart to let her know how much she meant to me as often as I possibly could.

I speak well of both of my parents to my children and to all I talk to concerning them. I honor my dad's memory and am now very grateful to him for his work ethic, his faith in God and all the wise counsel he gave me. Did I always agree with my mom on everything? No. Did I honor her for giving me life, a safe home and a Christian upbringing? Absolutely! I honored her. I expect my children to honor her. I simply do not tolerate from anyone a disrespectful attitude or action toward her. My mom was not perfect and she didn't claim to be. However, she was my mother and she is to be honored, period. Yahweh said so. That's all I need to know.

That brings us to a challenge that many of us do struggle with to one degree or another. Honoring our parents when there are things they do that seemingly should disqualify them. Men, hear me clearly on this matter. Honoring our parents has nothing to do with their deserving our honor. Honoring our parents is a heart matter of our obedience to our King. To honor them is not a suggestion made by Yahweh. It is a very firm instruction that He expects us to follow. This instruction is so important that he wrote it by his own fiery finger on those two stone tablets we call The Ten Commandments.

I've come to realize that it really doesn't matter if a parent deserves honor, or even how a parent responds to being honored. The key is that this principle is to be followed no matter what. Why? Because giving a parent honor has less to do about who they are and much more to do with becoming the man I need to be. If I cannot honor my parents, how will I ever be able to honor anyone else in my life?

With all this in mind, how do we honor our parents? Here are some ideas to get you started.

- When your parent enters the room, or your house, rise and go to greet them.

▢ When you enter their home or an event at which they have already arrived, seek them out and greet them first before greeting others.

▢ When you speak about your parents to others, especially to your children, focus on their strengths and the positive things they have done for you. (Look for the positive in them and in your circumstances with them. You will eventually find it.)

▢ Call your parents at least once a week, especially if you live a great distance from them. The conversation doesn't have to be lengthy. Simply let them know that you are thinking of them. (In a Hebrew perspective, it is the child's responsibility to "seek out" the parents, not the other way around.)

▢ Visit your parents as often as possible. Take them out for a meal or a cup of coffee.

▢ Remember a gift on Mother's Day and Father's Day, and their birthdays. In fact, surprise them with a gift even when there is no special occasion to warrant one.

▢ Ask for their advice on your concerns. They may have no experience in your field of work, or even in the details of your particular family or social situation. However, life has many common threads of truth and wisdom running through it that have nothing to do with the actual circumstances surrounding an issue. Those pearls of truth and wisdom are in our parents and they are usually happy to help with what they can, if we will ask them. (My Dad was a dairy farmer. I was an insurance agent before I entered ministry. I learned to ask my Dad for advice on all sorts of business- related issues. Even though he didn't know a thing about the insurance industry, his advice often helped me a great deal.)

- ☐ Ask your parents to speak a blessing over you and over your children. Let them know how very important this is to you. They may not understand this action completely; however they will be honored by your asking it of them.

- ☐ What about your spouse's parents? Do you honor them by calling them "Dad" and Mom"? Unless they have requested otherwise, you should. Hear me, men. Your dishonor of them dishonors your wife. You are telling her by your actions that the most influential and important people in her life are not worthy of your honor, and therefore that part of what makes her who she is to you holds no value. Men, this is a serious mistake and will damage your relationship with your wife and with her parents. Just as with your own parents, it doesn't matter how you feel about your in-laws or what they may or may not have done for you. They brought into this world and shaped the life of the most important person Yahweh has placed in your life. She would not be who she is to you without them. They deserve your honor on that basis alone.

- ☐ Concerning your wife once again, be absolutely sure she is given opportunity to visit "her father's house", her parents, as often as possible. I know this is difficult when your in-laws may live a great distance from you, however, this needs to be a priority in your budget and plans. Husbands, you are the one's commanded by Yahweh to "leave and cleave", not your wife. She will always need a close relationship with her parents. By your being sure she gets to "go home" as often as possible honors both her parents and her. Be smart!

»Honoring Those Who Lead and Mentor You

Who are the people (other than your parents and spouse) who have had or currently have the greatest impact on your life? I can think of many: my teachers, my pastor, those who have mentored me in various aspects of my life, my past employers and my friends who excel in areas that I do not. Those who are in governmental authority over me also impact my life.

Who is on your list? How do you honor them? Do you understand that your attitude toward and relationship with them reveals to Yahweh a great deal about your heart? Your attitude and conduct concerning them, with honor or with dishonor, determines your ability to grow, advance, gain authority of your own and receive honor from others. Even Yahweh reveals, "I will give to each one of you according to your works." (Revelation 2:23) He also tells us that when we are faithful in the small things, he can trust [honor] us with greater things. (Luke 19:17)

Not showing honor to those who lead and mentor you reveals a heart of arrogance and a self-serving attitude. This may be a new thought to some of you: a lack of giving honor is in itself an act of dishonor. Nothing shouts "it's all about me" louder than refusing to honor. Ignoring one who should be honored is also an act of dishonor. Let me ask you a few questions on a very practical note. When you arrive at your church do you seek out those who lead you and greet them with honor? When you are at an event where one who has mentored you is also in attendance, do you immediately and respectfully greet them? How do you honor them in the presence of others? How do you speak of them when they are not present? Have you done anything to show your appreciation to these key people of influence in your life?

Maybe you are asking, "Why is this so important anyway?" The answer is simple. Dishonoring those in roles of leadership in your life also reveals to Yahweh a heart of dishonor toward Him. Is He not the one who placed you in your position with these leaders and mentors? Could it be possible that your choice to dishonor them stems from a rebellious little corner in your heart toward Him?

Here's how you can tell. Have you ever heard yourself arguing with Yahweh like this? "God, what were you thinking? You obviously had no idea what you were doing when you gave me this job, placed me in this congregation, gave me these friends, gave me this mentor... Well, I will just adjust these mistakes and follow after what I think is the right instruction, the right move, the right person that thinks more like I do. I'm sure you won't mind." Guys, if you truly heard Yahweh when you stepped into these positions and relationships to begin with, you had better shut down that dishonorable train of thoughts and attitudes real fast. You are about to do serious damage to yourself.

Men, Yahweh knows good and well that if He does not place us in positions and relationships that will challenge and sharpen us, we simply will stagnate and will never be able to reach our full potential. Does your pastor rub you the wrong way sometimes? Are there days that your mentor seems to be asking too much of you? Do you have a leader that does not agree with your opinion? Don't complain. Don't grumble to others about him behind his back. Rather, choose to honor that person in every way that you can, and then do your best to discover just what it is in you that Yahweh is trying to change for the better.

Men, dishonor at its very root is simply rebellion. It will cause you to negate or belittle the important role of other people Yahweh has placed in your life. In worst case scenarios, that wicked little root of a rebellious spirit will even cause you to attack, hurt, and "murder" these people with your words and actions. Men, we need to understand that pride (arrogance) truly does precede a fall. Pride will cause us to dishonor others. Dishonoring others will eventually destroy us.

As you study the Book of Proverbs, you will come to understand that honor and obedience to instruction brings prosperity. Employers cannot and will not treat all employees the same. Put yourself in their position. How would you honor loyalty, diligence in performing the work assigned, and an attitude that isn't constantly watching the clock for quitting time? Only the diligent are placed in authority and only authority can give recognition to the diligent. Men, if you cannot follow an instruction from your employer, if you cannot stick to company policies and procedures, then you are by your actions telling your employer that you simply cannot be trusted. Your boss most likely is not going to argue with you or say a word about your dishonor. Your boss simply will not promote you to a higher position. Your boss might simply hold back that raise in pay you were hoping for. Your boss may even choose to let you go.

Remember, the key to your success in life will be determined by who you choose to honor and who you choose to dishonor. Be polite. Do not talk negatively about your boss behind their back. Don't take advantage of the benefits they provide. Guard them as the privilege that they are. Do what you can to build up your employer and his/her business. Thank them for giving you the opportunity to work for them. Their success will bring abundance to you. Their failure will leave you without a job.

Employers, you are likewise expected to honor your employees. If you have chosen wisely, your employees will bring great increase to your life. They enter your business with skills, abilities, and gifts that will help you accomplish your purpose and vision. Honor those who work in diligence and respect those who make every effort to respect you. Reward good performance. Promote those who have earned your trust. Honor your employees by giving them a good and safe work environment. Provide them with the tools and resources they need to accomplish the work that you expect from them. Help them develop their work and leadership skills. Speak well of your employees; don't tear them down behind their backs or tear them apart with badly worded correction. Respect your employees and they will respect you. Honor them and they will be the key to your business success.

Guys, the same practical steps of showing honor apply in the churches and ministries Yahweh has place you in. Look for qualities in your church family and in your pastor that you admire. Focus on their strengths, abilities, and positive attributes. Be grateful, encouraging and helpful. When you see weakness, and you will, view what you see as an opportunity to show loving arms of compassion and help, not a chance to judge and criticize. Rather than criticize and tear down, ask "How may I serve?" A choice to honor and serve will help you uproot any arrogance that may be blindsiding you and help you truly appreciate what those leading your congregation deal with in their work on a day to day basis.

Please understand that Yahweh, not man, has placed your pastor in his position of leadership. Trust Yahweh to correct His appointed ones. Keep in mind a simple principle: we most quickly see the faults in others that we ourselves possess. Viewing the struggles of others as positively as you can will help you discover ways that you can also improve yourself. Learn to pray for your spiritual leaders. They need to step more fully into their destinies, just as you do!

I also want to encourage you, men, to look upon your life past and present. Identify those who have positively impacted your life. Seriously, make a list. Has someone gone out of their way to give you their time and favor? Is there someone in your life that is always there to encourage you; that sees your aches and pains and longs to help you? Is there someone, past or present, who has crossed mountains and wilderness with you just to see you succeed? Who are those people in your life that are always there, looking to help you even with the small things? Find some way to honor and reward them. If it is at all possible, give each person a phone call or send them a simple card to tell them how much you value what they have contributed to your life. Take them out for coffee or a nice meal.

Perhaps Yahweh will also nudge you to send a gift or a financial blessing to them. Be quick to obey that instruction, because Yahweh is trying to help you open a window through which He in turn can bless you!

On the flipside, in your reflections, you may also identify people that you now understand that you have dishonored. The instruction is the same: a phone call, a simple card. Apologize, ask their forgiveness and offer restitution. Dishonor robs people. The Torah teaches that the one who has robbed must make restitution usually 20% above the value of what was taken. Your goal is to restore honor in that relationship. The relationship may be beyond repair, but honor by restitution can still be restored. Perhaps flowers, a gift card, a meal out, a return of any items that were taken (plus 20% of their value), a gift of money, tickets to an event they would enjoy; whatever you know you need to do, do it. Restore honor! (This instruction applies to every relationship in your life, including a stranger.)

»*Honoring Your Wife and Children*

I am going to go into much more detail on these important people in your life later in this book. For now, let me simply stress to you that your ability to honor your wife and your children are key to creating and sustaining an atmosphere of true peace in your home. Honestly, much that applies to honoring Yahweh, your parents and those in leadership in your life readily applies to your wife and children as well.

Listen to them. Communicate with them. Value them for who they are. Verbally acknowledge the good characteristics, talents and skills you see in them. Celebrate their special days. Spend set apart time with them during each week. Give them simple gifts for no other reason than to see them smile. Speak only good of them to others. Encourage them. Ask forgiveness when you need to and make restitution, as well. Pray over them and bless them. Such a man is easy for them to honor in return!

Honor is enormous in the Kingdom of Yahweh. Everything in His realm revolves around it. Honor will open doors that cannot be opened by intelligence, education and the best of talents and skills. Honor is the key to a good life in every possible way. There are so many Scriptures that teach and exemplify honor that I can't even begin to list them for you in this book. If I must choose only one with which to close this chapter and encourage you with, it is found in Ephesians. May each of us as Yahweh's Real Men aspire to Paul's words.

Therefore, stripping off falsehood let everyone speak truth with his neighbor, because we are intimately related to each other as parts of a body. Be angry, but don't sin – don't let the sun go down before you have dealt with the cause of your anger; otherwise you leave room for the Adversary. The thief must stop stealing; instead, he should make an honest living by his own efforts. This way he will be able to share with those in need. Let no harmful language come to your mouth, only good words that are helpful in meeting the need, words that will benefit those who hear them. Don't cause grief to God's Ruach HaKodesh [Holy Spirit], for he has stamped you as his property until the day of final redemption. Get rid of all bitterness, rage, anger, violent assertiveness and slander, along with all spitefulness. Instead, be kind to each other, tenderhearted; and forgive each other, just as in the Messiah God has also forgiven you. **Ephesians 4:25-29**

Chapter Four:
Becoming a Better Husband

We all desire peace or "shalom" in our homes. Such peace means much more than the absence of strife. Shalom means completeness, as in having everything one needs to accomplish what Yahweh has called him to be and do. For a husband, to bring peace to his life and home is the greatest accomplishment Yahweh's Real Man can achieve.

Shalom in the home is only possible when there is honor in the home. That is exactly why it is so very important for us as men to understand what honor is and choose to practice it. In the home, honor begins with your spouse; that wonderful woman that you fell head over in heels in love with and chose to marry. Marriage is a lifelong covenant, men, not a contract that can be broken. A word to the wise among us: if you want a happy, lifelong covenant relationship with your wife you must choose to honor her.

Honor is very important to your wife. Here's a little tip that will go a long way to helping all of us be better husbands. A wife will often tell her husband that she wants to know that he loves her. What is she really asking for? Yes, she likes your genuine words and the warm fuzzies. All women do. However, love is much more than words and warm fuzzies. It is far more than an emotion. Love is honor and respect put into action in every aspect of your marriage relationship. Love requires putting her needs ahead of my own. Without this, all the attempts in the universe at romance and warm fuzzies will mean absolutely nothing to her. Warm, sexual response to her husband will be shortcoming from a wife when she feels disrespected or has been dishonored in any way.

Here is a simple exercise for all of us, men. Reconsider the following Scriptures using the word "honor" every time you read the word "love".

> *Husbands, love (honor) your wives, just as Messiah also loved (honored) the church and gave Himself for her.* **Ephesians 5:25**

> *So husbands ought to love (honor) their own wives as their own bodies; he who loves (honors) his wife loves (honors) himself.* **Ephesians 5:28**

> *Husbands, love (honor) your wives and do not be bitter toward them.* **Colossians 3:19**

I admit that there was a time in my life not that long ago that I did not equate honor with love. I never considered that the two were connected. What a difference a little revelation can make! I have come to understand that the richest spiritual resource I can give my wife's soul is honor. To honor her is to give life to her in the deepest regions of her being. She knows that she is valued and loved. She knows that I believe in her just as she is and want to help her become everything Yahweh has created her to be. I want to honor and champion her in every way that I possibly can. Isn't that what Messiah does for His Bride, men? We are to do no less for our brides.

As a pastor, I have come to realize that most wives suffer from a serious lack of honor from their husbands. This has come to grieve me. I see so many great couples who are so close to having incredible marriages yet miss that mark simply because the husband does not know how to honor his wife.

In fact, these men are often the biggest source of dishonor in their wives lives. How so? Whether intentional or not, they are a constant source of criticism and belittlement to them. Now, let me preface that by saying that this kind of behavior is not always evident in public. However, any time I meet a woman without her hubby by her side who constantly complains about her husband my first thought is "I wonder if this woman's husband is failing to honor her?" I wonder if she has become broken by his constant negative comments and criticisms. Let me explain the dynamic in this situation.

Guys, women are not wired to handle negative comments, sharp words, and criticism even in jest and certainly not in a burst of anger. We men, on the other hand are wired to deal with such challenges and attacks as a part of the reality of our everyday interaction with the world. We understand such things to be a part of the competitive nature of life and we are often motivated to improvement by this process. Women, though no less strong and poised to improve themselves, respond better to other forms of challenges, many of which would take us men out in a single blow.

When a husband is critical and speaks snide comments toward his wife, even if he thinks they are funny, those words will affect his marriage dramatically. When a woman is negatively critiqued or criticized, her self-worth comes under attack. Her confidence level drops and insecurities can quickly set in, freezing her emotionally and even damaging her health. When a husband criticizes his wife, she begins to question her understanding of him. If he loves her, why would he attack her? She will begin to shut out his voice on everything simply as a means to protect herself. Because she is experiencing his remarks as inconsiderate and dishonoring, she will also begin to respond to him in like manner. She will become easily agitated by and displeased with everything that he says or does.

Yahweh has seemingly wired women to have zero-tolerance for criticism and harshness from their husbands. Wise is the husband who understands this and learns to phrase his words of correction and encouragement in a positive, tender fashion. Men, always refrain from sharp, cutting remarks or criticism, even if you are trying to be cute or funny. It is not appreciated by the woman in your life.

If criticism and attack have become a part of your response when you are disappointed or angered by something she has said or done, step away from the situation for as long as it takes and reground yourself. Think about how to express your anger or frustration with words and mannerisms that honor her but still address the issue at hand. Do not risk crushing the most priceless person in your life. Breaking her spirit will cost you dearly. Better to keep your mouth shut until you can handle your words with wisdom and honor.

The ancient Jewish sages have come to a great understanding of this critical dynamic in a marriage. They teach that a wife is designed by Yahweh to be a mirror to her husband. What a husband sees as unsettling words or behavior in his wife is simply what his wife is reflecting of himself back to him. In other words, men, quite often what our wife is reacting to is something in us, not in herself. She most likely can't even explain why she is doing or saying what she is in that moment. She is simply reacting to something she is consciously or subconsciously seeing in you.

The day I understood that my wife is my mirror literally changed our marriage forever. It has changed me as well. This revelation that what I complain to my wife about, thinking that she is at fault, is usually something that is lacking in me now causes me to choose to better respond not only to her but also to my heavenly Father. I realize that when she is manifesting a behavior that seems disrespectful or dishonoring toward me it is usually because of one of two reasons: 1) I have failed to place honor and respect in to her, therefore she cannot reflect such back to me, or 2) I have an unresolved issue between myself and my heavenly Father that she is merely reflecting back to me as I look at her. In either case, my wife is wired by Creator Yahweh to pick up on what is wrong and shine it right back into my face. Men, understand this, she is not able to shut off this part of who she is just because it makes you uncomfortable.

She has no choice in this matter because that is exactly what Yahweh designed her to do.

You see, men, our wives are Creator-designed incubators. That is how He designed women to function and not just in bearing children. What I place in my wife she will nurture, multiply, and return to me. That includes both the good and the bad. Whatever you place in your wife will come back to you, stronger and with greater intensity than the original you placed in her.

This truth is at first a bit intimidating to embrace. Yet, this is also Yahweh's great design in how to help us become better men. This is exactly why He calls our wives our "helpmates". Being our helpmate is not just about physical work and raising a family, side by side. This also means that He is going to use her to sharpen and improve me to help me become what He intends me to be.

When my wife acts up in rebellion toward me it is almost always a huge bill board sign from Yahweh saying, "Steve, you had better look at what is going on inside of you. There is something you and I need to deal with immediately." I have learned to keep my mouth shut in response to her challenges or emotional outbursts until I have come before my Father and asked Him to show me my heart. I am astonished at how often she had every right to respond as she did. She was being my mirror so that Yahweh could get me to deal with something he wanted to see change in me. Remarkable. My wife truly is a gift from Father!

Why did Creator Yahweh design women this way? Let's be honest with ourselves, men. How many men do you know that are capable of seeing themselves correctly? Consider how differently men and women approach standing in front of a real mirror. Women usually see what needs to be changed and improved. They see the extra few pounds, the graying hair, a new wrinkle, and sags where there weren't any before the children were born. Men, on the other hand, run their fingers through their hair (if they still have any), pull their pants up by the belt, suck in the gut, check out their profiles left and right, maybe even pump up those muscles if no one is looking and walk away thinking to themselves, "Yes! I still got it!" This may be funny to think about but it is our truth, guys.

This is the same mentality that allows us to walk into a messy room and not see the mess, a thing that frustrates most women to no end! They are wired to see what is out of whack. We are not. That is why we need them to show us. We shouldn't criticize our wives for doing exactly what we need them to do. The only way most of us can honestly see ourselves is by the mirrors called our wives.

That very same ability of women to see what is out of whack is also exactly why they do not need us critiquing and criticizing them. They usually see their own shortcomings and problems very well. In fact, what they need most from us is to not allow them to sink themselves with what they already see. Yahweh wants the husband to correct himself, not his wife. As he allows Yahweh to change him, she will readily adjust.

There is another interesting Hebrew perspective that I would like you to give some thought to regarding your wife. The Jewish sages believe that YHVH's Word does not obligate a woman to marry. She can live on her own and usually will do quite well on her own. This is why at the death of a wife most men either remarry very quickly or die within in a short time period. Women will live for years, often decades, after the death of a spouse. This is also why a divorced man will often quickly remarry while a divorced woman may take years or choose to never remarry. A man is wired to be married. Women can do just fine without us. Sobering thought, isn't it?

The sages do believe that men are the ones commanded to marry, be fruitful and multiply. Why? Because a woman is easily corrected by Yahweh. Her heart is wired to respond to a husband and, as her ultimate Husband, Yahweh can easily touch her heart with great effect. She walks the earth open to His correction. She is by His design a nurturer and will seek to create and multiply whatever is placed in her hands. She is wired to multiply and to give so that she can make life better for herself and for everyone that becomes a part of her life. (This is also why woman have remarkable business potential.) She needs little to no prompting to do this. She also walks the earth to fulfill another specific purpose: to facilitate the correction of her husband's soul, should Yahweh give her a spouse. She is a remarkable tool in His hands to cause you to become a righteous man.

Hear me, gentlemen. I am going to say it again because you must never forget this. Men need women. Women do not need men. She can survive and, in fact, do quite well without you and deep inside she knows it. She may be devastated for a time at losing you, whether by death or divorce. But she will make it through, especially if left as the primary caregiver for her children. Husband, know and understand this. Your wife chooses to be with you.

Men, if you are married or hoping to get married, this issue of honoring your wife is the most important trait you can possibly develop. Our wives are gifts from a Father who loves us and is deeply concerned about our character as His men upon His earth. When we dishonor our wives by constantly critiquing and criticizing them, blaming them for what we refuse to take responsibility for in our words and actions, we crush them. We break the mirror Yahweh made her to be in our life, and in doing so, seriously hamper growth in our own relationship with Him. She was placed in your life to help that relationship become all that it is meant to be. Dishonor her and we rob ourselves! Dishonor, in Yahweh's Kingdom, will disqualify us from the financial, physical, emotional, and spiritual blessings He has waiting for us. Such honor from Him is only given to those who choose to give honor to others, period.

As the men who are the leaders in our homes, we also need to understand that the most powerful way we can teach honor to our children, especially our sons is to model it with our wives. When Dad openly honors Mom, it speaks volumes to the children. Our sons need to learn how to honor a woman so that one day they will be able to honor their wives. Our daughters need to see Dad honor Mom so they understand they are worthy of honor as women and should never settle for anything less in their own marriages.

Honoring your wife also communicates to them that they too need to honor and respect mom and each other. Our children must learn from their fathers that a human soul, no matter whom, is of greatest value to Yahweh and that no one should violate a soul with dishonor and disrespect at any time. The lesson of honor is most powerfully taught by how you respond to and treat your wife. As with all things in our homes, what goes on there is not about us. It is about our children, grandchildren, and the generations that will follow them.

I firmly believe that if a man does not know how to sincerely honor his wife, his most precious human relationship, then it is very unlikely that he is truly able to honor his pastor or rabbi, his employer or employees, his parents, or even Yahweh himself. Men, we need to learn honor and how to give it. Shalom in our homes, our churches, and the culture of our communities and our nation is depending on us to do so now as never before. Our lessons in honor need to begin with our wives. She is your mirror. If she is not reflecting honor toward you, then guess where it is missing?

> *Just as water reflects the face, so one human heart reflects another.* **Proverbs 27:19**

Over the many centuries, Jewish men have learned that when a man honors his wife, things go well with him. There is a spiritual dimension to the honor of a man towards his wife that even the Apostle Peter taught.

You husbands, likewise, conduct your married lives with understanding. Although your wife may be weaker physically, you should respect her as a fellow-heir of the gift of Life. If you don't, your prayers will be blocked. **I Peter 3:7**

I sometimes wonder if we as men truly understand the significance of this teaching. Respect and honor go hand in hand. Our wives are joint heirs with us. They are not in any way shape or form inferior to us in Yahweh's Kingdom. She has been given equal standing in the sight of the Almighty in regards to His gift of Life. She has been gifted and is treasured by Him just as we as men are. To treat her with dishonor and disrespect is to dishonor and disrespect the Father. She is His workmanship just as much as we men are.

Here's the question that gets to the rub of what Peter is telling us as husbands. Do you have unanswered prayers, men? In fact, are you even wondering if your prayers are reaching His ears? If we are disrespecting and dishonoring our wives the teaching is very clear. Our prayers are blocked. Men, how we treat our wives is not an issue Yahweh takes lightly. We will and do pay for it. Turn this issue of respect and honor toward your wife around and He will hear and answer you once again. Choosing not to do so simply leaves you out there in life on your own. That is not a good place to be, ever.

I also want to remind you of Friday evenings and the Sabbath practice of Hebrew men blessing their wives. Men, speak a blessing to your wife as often as possible. Do this every day if you can, but at least once a week. I mentioned earlier that Hebrew men recite Proverbs 31 over their wives as they bless them. Any of us can do that; it is not that hard! I encourage you to make it personal. Use her name as you read these verses over her. Replace "she" with "you". Build her up with these words. They will help her to understand how remarkable she truly is designed to be.

In the same breath, I also encourage you to personally, as a man, take the time to go over Proverbs 31 so that you can gain a greater appreciation for who your wife is designed by Creator Yahweh to be. She is a remarkable creation and any husband worth his salt should be asking himself, "Am I preventing my wife in any way from becoming a Proverbs 31 woman?" This is a powerful question to ask yourself, because if you are preventing her you are treading on dangerous ground. How so? You are manipulating her life to be what you want it to be, not what Yahweh designed her to be. I would not want to be you standing before our King in that area of accountability.

With that understanding, guys, I want to give you some practical advice on how to honor your wife as the one in your relationship that "manages her household well". There are three actions that will greatly dishonor and harm your wife. One is failing to provide for her the tools and funds she needs to manage the home and nurture the children especially if it leaves her feeling unprotected or insecure. The second is undermining her efforts to keep things in "check and balance" regarding how the household is being managed day by day. The third is having complete lack of interest or concern in how she manages the household day by day.

Men, our Creator-given role is to be the primary provider for our families and households. We do ourselves, our wives and our children, a tremendous dishonor when we chose to not fulfill that role. In a Biblical community, this is simply not acceptable. Your wife and children are to be provided and cared for above and before anything else. Whether you have a great marriage or have been divorced, this standard does not change. Men, you remain responsible for your children regardless. You also are responsible to be sure your wife, or ex-wife, is not out living on the street, homeless. Yahweh does not take the mistreatment of women and children lightly at all. Even if a man calls himself a member of His

Kingdom, if he fails to provide for his wife or children, he is guilty of a blatant dishonor of their value before Yahweh. This man is to be considered to be worse than a heathen. This man will be held accountable before Yahweh and, according to both the Torah and the Apostle Paul, should be held to account by the community of believers as well. He must correct his lack of action, period.

In a good marriage, husbands, you need to be sure your wife has what she needs to fulfill her role as manager of the household and nurturer to your children. Be involved in shaping the budget she needs to run the house and do your best to see that the budget stays funded. When appliances, large or small, break down, do your best to have them repaired or replaced quickly. Have the children outgrown their shoes? Be sure she has the funds to meet that need.

Your wife has the full ability to contribute financially to the household as well. The Proverbs 31 wife deals in real estate, agriculture and an in-home business. She is free to contribute financially according to her time and skills. However, she is looking to you to be the *primary* source, as well she should be. (My wife likes to point out that the Proverbs 31 woman "manages her maid servants well" and asks, "When do I get to have maidservants, Steve?!") Do not frustrate and dishonor her by leaving her without the means to manage the home.

Let's address the details of the day to day managing of the household a bit more. Guys, be careful not to undermine your wife's plans and efforts in the home. Your usurpation of her management of the daily household says to her that you do not feel she is adequate to do her job well. When you arrive home from work, do not put your foot down and take over. Instead, ask her what her plan is (what to make for dinner, timing the children's homework and bedtimes, needed urgent home repairs and improvements, etc.) then come alongside to help her carry out that plan. Discuss your observations and ideas, but do not criticize or change her plans or take over any aspect of what is going on, unless of course, she asks you to.

Hear me, men of honor! The house and all that goes on there is "her turf". Your responsibilities are outside the home in the workplace and as a leader in the community. Your wife has the pulse, the ebb and flow, of the household constantly on her radar and usually will have a better understanding of the full scope of what is going on day by day than you do. (Amazingly, this is also often still true if she works outside the home. How women can do that is beyond me!) Honor that incredible ability in her. Be aware that if you bring constant disruptions into that "ebb and flow" of the household day after day, it will also bring sure chaos into your marriage. Because she feels disrespected, your wife will lose her ability to trust you with the details of her life. Remember, she is a mirror. If she receives your words and actions as disrespect, disrespect toward you will easily set in. Respect her Biblical position as the day to day manager of the household and you will rise up in her regard considerably!

Men, we need to be honest about ourselves. Managing an entire household is not an easy task and requires a skill set men do not usually have. Your wife does. She has the remarkable ability to multi-task household management issues in the midst of constant interruptions, managing the relationships between the children and with you, and still maintaining the wherewithal to see how every detail of a day and a week must flow together for the common benefit of the family. She can adjust things on a moment's notice and still get it all done. She can do all of this at any given moment of any day or night. Do not take her remarkable abilities for granted for a single moment. Compliment her on every accomplishment at home. Provide direction and insight, but do not step in and take over unless an emergency deems it necessary.

On the flip side, do not disconnect from your wife's management of the household either. Stay aware of what is going on. Ask her to communicate to you the needs of the house and of the children, listen to her desires in how to meet those needs, be involved in the monthly budgeting and overall financial scenario of the household. Every morning – yes, *every morning* - ask her how you can help in any area and then follow through as soon as possible.

As you work together to fashion a plan and template for how you both desire to see your mutual home managed and the children nurtured, your ability to honor her in her unique and high calling as a wife and mother is crucial to dissolving the potential for an invasion of chaos and conflict. To have shalom (peace) in the home, honor is the key.

Earlier in this chapter, I stated that love is honor and respect put into action. Beyond what I have already shared, some of you might be wondering what that looks like for your wife. Let me make a few practical suggestions to get you started. Hopefully this will help you come up with more on your own. Guys, you can also simply ask your wife what you can do to honor her. You might be surprised at the simplicities in her answer.

☐ First and most important, commit to never speak harsh words to or criticize your wife again, never again, period. If you are angry, back away and cool off. Rethink how you will say what you need to say politely and gently.

☐ Create a private time for the two of you away from the children and all distractions. Use that time to tell her that you now understand that Yahweh has given her to you to be your mirror. Give her permission to speak constructively and positively into your life. Ask her to tell you when she is feeling unsettled, stressed or fearful at any time. Help her to understand how to talk to you in a way that you know that you can receive from her.

- Learn to rephrase back to her any critiques she has for you in a way that allows her to explore and express what she has said to you and why. Remember, the desire of her heart is to help you, not hurt you. It is your responsibility to create a safe space in your marriage for her to fulfill her function.

- Commit to take responsibility for your own words and actions. Never again blame your wife for your failures or shortcomings.

- When your wife speaks to you, actively listen. Turn off the television or video game. Silence the cell phone. Walk away from the computer. Put down your hobby. Look at her face to face and affirm that you are hearing her words.

- Compliment her in front of others, especially the children. It's not hard. Maybe it's her hair, her smile, the delicious meal she made for the family, anything that you truly do appreciate about her at that moment. She needs to hear how important she is to you and that you value what she contributes to your life.

- Acknowledge her accomplishments and achievements in front of others, especially the children. Let her know that you value her dedication and efforts, and that you are proud of her.

- Use your manners! Say "please" and "thank you". Open doors for her. Help her with her coat. Carry things for her. Say "excuse me" when you should. Be polite. Remember, oh mighty kings in His Kingdom, that she is the queen the King of Kings has placed by your side. Treat her like one.

- Honor her with unexpected gifts. They do not have to be elaborate or expensive, simply something you know she will enjoy or something that she desires. Flowers, dinner out, an unplanned drive to a favorite location, jewelry, a music cd, tickets to the ballet, a weekend away, etc. (Tip: If you are doing the actions of honor already mentioned, she will not be suspicious that you are trying to cover up for something!)

☐ See to her physical needs with a commitment to help her always be at her best. Clothing, jewelry, shoes, items that she needs to run the household efficiently and care for the children, anything that she needs to fulfill her calling as a wife, a mother, and a woman. Be quick to repair what is broken and replace what cannot be repaired. (Yeshua faithfully equips his Bride with all she needs to fulfill her calling. We need to do the same for our Brides.)

☐ If your wife works part-time or full-time outside the home, help her with the housework and laundry. This tells her that her time and energy level is important to you. This also tells her that you willingly accept responsibility for the space that you together call "home". As the old adage goes, "Many hands make light work". The more that you help her, the more time and energy she will have to give to being your loving companion. (Yes – that does include sex.)

☐ Always keep in mind that she is "the household manager". Honor her by honoring her plans in the home day by day and week by week. Remember that she has the pulse of the entire family and household on her radar. Trust her instincts in these matters. Yahweh wired her to fulfill this role.

☐ Absolutely insist that your children respect and honor your wife. This is true in blended families as well as natural families. There may be days your children do not like you or your wife; that is normal. However, they need to honor and respect you and her regardless of what they think or feel. Guard her honor at all times, even with your parents, your siblings, and other extended-family relatives. She will readily guard your honor likewise.

▢ Honor your wife by honoring her talents and gifts. Be sure that in her very busy roles of wife and mother that she has an active outlet to use them. This is especially true of young women who stay at home with young children. She needs to actively be who she is in these areas of her life or she will lose her sense of self-worth and self-esteem. Family life demands a great deal of giving on a woman's part. Be sure that she has that positive inflow that comes from doing things that hold deep meaning to her as often as possible. Be sure this is *her* time, without the children or even you, in tow. Honor her by guarding and building up her unique identity.

Again, these are just a few principles, thoughts and insights to get you started on the rewarding road of honoring your wife. If you sincerely have no idea what compliments, actions, or gifts your wife would appreciate - if you have no idea what her gifts, interests, and dreams are - then you had better immediately get down to the business of getting to know your wife again. You fell in love with her because of those very specific things. They make her who she is. Be sure that you are not guilty of crushing them out of her life. She is a remarkable treasure of a person. She has to be, because "God don't make junk!" This is especially true of the incredible women that are in lives of the Real Men of Yahweh. Amen!

Chapter Five:
Becoming a Better Father

In my own journey through life, my Heavenly Father loves me so much that He doesn't hesitate to provide me with an occasional "wake-up calls" so that I can adjust my walk when needed. One of those wake-up calls took place a few years back as I and my family were heading to Denver, Colorado for a ministry leadership seminar.

The seminar was scheduled to start on Sunday morning, but because our Saturdays (the Sabbath) are full of church ministry, we were not able to leave our home for the 9 hour drive to Denver until 7 PM. Because I don't sleep a whole lot to begin with, I was fully prepared to drive a majority of what would be an overnight trip.

My wife was very tired from the day's activities but stayed awake until around 10:00. She finally gave in to her exhaustion, put a pillow behind her head and nodded off. Our son had already stretched out on the back seat and was sound asleep. So that both could rest soundly, I chose not to listen to any music or teachings as we traveled through the Wyoming night.

Around midnight I started to feel a bit sleepy. I knew that Sunday would be a full and busy day, so I determined to press on as the driver so that Evelyn and Matthew could get as much sleep as possible. Being of the stubborn German heritage that I am, I reasoned that I was just fine. I opened the window a crack to let the cool night air blow on my face and kept moving.

I'm not sure when I dosed off or for how long. All I know is that at some point the sound of the tires bumping across the ribs carved into the highway shoulders filled the car. Evelyn was the first to wake up and yelled, "Steve!" Up to that point, I was still asleep. She grabbed the steering wheel and pulled us back on the road just before we hit the guard rail.

Finally fully awake, I at looked at my wife. I will never forget the look on her face. Her hand was still firmly grasping the wheel while a mix of fear, anger and panic revealed everything in her in that very moment. "I got it now, honey," was all I could say. Her hand relaxed and dropped from the wheel. She didn't say a word.

With adrenalin now pulsing through my body, I glanced in the rear view mirror to check on my son. He was sitting up, wide awake, his face covered with fear. Unsure of what had just happened, a questioning look on his face peered back at me. In that moment, Evelyn finally spoke.

"Why didn't you pull over and wake me up?! I could have driven for an hour or more so you could get some sleep. I am fully able to help you shoulder the burden of getting us to Denver. Steve, you could have killed all three of us!"

Her anger was vivid and she had every right to it. I was angry too. What had I risked by trying to go past my own limits? I had put my family's safety in serious jeopardy because I thought I knew what I was doing. Of course, I knew better. I was tired. I should have stopped. That was a stupid decision, just plain stupid. I was beating myself up pretty well.

I was now wide awake again. In fact, I was physically shaking. I glanced at Evelyn. So was she. I kept driving. Matthew was still sitting up, not about to go back to sleep. His eyes were glued to the road. For several minutes, none of us said another word. Finally, I was calm enough to apologize to both of them. I was very sorry for endangering both of their lives. That was so very wrong of me.

I also asked my Father for forgiveness. I was not taking good care of those He had given to me. I started reflecting on the path that led to my falling asleep at the wheel. The lull of the road had caused me to stop paying attention to details. The speed of the car kept propelling me forward, even though I was missing some basic steps. I was determined to get there without anyone's help. Had Evelyn not woke me up and grabbed the wheel while she screamed, we would have perished.

The parallels to the rest of my life as a husband and father came rolling in at me like a tidal wave. It wasn't just on this drive to Denver that I had fallen asleep. I was appalled as Father began to show me the other areas in my life that I was "falling asleep at the wheel." My busyness and misguided priorities were causing me to seriously lack in not taking care of my family in certain areas of their basic needs. These were needs as a husband and father that I knew I was responsible for.

It dawned on me that even though I was a pastor and well-schooled in the Word of God, I was really not that different than 99% of the other men I knew. All of us are running hard, not paying attention to the details, often just doing things to get them done with no effort put into finding out how to do them better. I had a destination to reach, and I didn't give much thought to who I was putting at risk in my selfish efforts to get there.

There is a wise adage out there that states, "The definition of insanity is continuing to do things the same way but expecting different results." As I looked at my life and my family, I realized that what I was doing was insane. In a moment of brutal honesty with myself, I realized I had no clue on how to be a Biblical husband to my wife or father to my children. I knew the Christian status quo, but I suddenly wanted more than that. No one had taught me how to truly bless my family or how to honor them as they so needed. I wanted to know what Yahweh instructs about being a man in His Kingdom.

At age 59, all it took was this "wake-up call" on an all-night road trip to Denver to turn my outlook on life and its purpose totally around. I finally saw the holes in my own life and, together, Father and I began to fill them in with His Truth.

Tragically, my story reflects the state of many families today. In fact, in some cases their stories are careening them toward fatality in their own relationships even more than mine did. I challenge each of you, men, to slow down and look at your life. Have you has fallen asleep at the wheel? Are you one of those Dads that made a choice to allow the long bumpy journey of life lull him into a comfortable slumber, free from the responsibility of actually driving the car? Even though this man may see himself "in the driver's seat", his wife has her hand on the steering wheel doing all that she can to protect and save her family. He may have put the gas in the car, but now that it is on the road, he has lost all desire, understanding and ability concerning how to drive the car. After all, she has it under control, doesn't she? He can watch TV and play his video games, bury himself in his work (secular or ministry), spend free time out with his buddies, or allow himself to be trapped in the tragic grasp of pornography. His household may be scraping hard against the guard rail, but they haven't driven off the cliff, yet.

Some fathers have abandoned the driver's seat altogether. In fact, they aren't even in the car with their families. They have left all of the driving to mom and the kids are in the back seat with no one really watching over them. Mom can't do her best with them because she has to keep her eyes focused on the highway. She is busy avoiding the crashes with her eyes set on what will hopefully be a safe and good destination. She sees and hears the turmoil in the back seat, but she is pretty much helpless as long as the car keeps moving. She's had to do the packing, the fueling up, plan the route and do the driving all on her own. As much as she loves her children and wants the best for them, she is not enjoying the trip.

In fact, neither of these moms is enjoying the trip. Neither are the children. They know that they are unprotected and without the leadership they so need and desire. There is a sense of abandonment, even anger and resentment, which is right there under the surface of their daily lives. How can they possibly honor and love this man who is simply not there for them physically, emotionally or spiritually? Their question is, "Will Dad wake up in time to put on the brakes and get us properly back on the road again?" They pray that he will, but in the meantime they will do their best (positively or negatively) to try to get his attention while trying to survive the ride.

Men, it is not too late! The most significant part of our calling as men is to be in driver's seat with our families. Many of us as followers of Yeshua already know that. Our challenge is that while most of us have the desire to fulfill that role, most of us have no idea how to. This does not have to be the case and that indeed is good news.

Where do we turn for instruction? I have great news for you! The answers are already there for us. They are found in Yahweh's Word: the Torah. The remainder of the Old Testament and also the New Testament, simply reinforce what God gave to the men of Israel at Mt. Sinai. His instruction guides us on how to function as good husbands and fathers.

In this chapter, I am going to do my best to help you grab hold of just a handful of good instruction on fatherhood from the One who is our perfect Father. We can learn so very much from Him. After all, He designed us to be men, husbands, and fathers. We do not have to abandon that design simply because we are afraid or clueless. Would He not be happy to help us learn how to best fulfill our destiny? Most emphatically, YES.

From the very beginning of earth and time as we know it, Yahweh's design for mankind was based upon on a divine goal: to see His Kingdom established upon the earth and function as it does in heaven. He created and placed mankind upon this planet to fulfill that goal. His purpose shapes our destiny, both as men and women. He created us to first have a meaningful relationship with Him, and then to have the same with one another. This is why He instructs us that we are to love him with all of our hearts, minds, and resources and also to love one another in the same manner.

Without these life giving relationships, mankind's life on earth would fall miserably short of the goal of literally creating heaven on earth. Yahweh describes this desired state like this. "I will put my tabernacle among you, and I will not reject you, but I will walk among you and be your God, and you will be my people." (Leviticus 26:11-12. See also Jeremiah 31:34, Ezekiel 37:27, Hebrews 10:11 and Revelation 21:3.) No matter what we do for work, pleasure or in raising our families, all of our actions and relationships are to move us and those around us closer to this highest desire becoming an everlasting reality in our lives.

Fathers, how then do we raise our children to step into this remarkable destiny? Let's start our pursuit of this goal with first gaining an understanding who our children are. Then, we will look at what our relationship to them is to be like and how we can achieve being a good father.

Children are a Blessing from Yahweh

Yahweh designed the family to be a blessing to the earth. He gave man a life-long covenant companion and partner in a woman. Together they were to bring more lives into the world and raise those children to be set apart from all other creation; men and women among whom God could walk and fellowship. As a family, they were to make the earth fruitful and prosper in their homes. In the context of this divine design, the people of Yahweh could truly say...

> *Behold, children are a heritage from the Lord, the fruit of the womb is a reward. Like arrows in the hand of a warrior, so are the children of one's youth. Happy is the man who has his quiver full of them.* **Psalm 127:3-5**

> *Your wife shall be like a fruitful vine in the very heart of your house, your children like olive plants all around your table. Behold, thus shall the man be blessed who fears the Lord.* **Psalm 128:3-4**

> *Children's children are the crown of old men, and the glory of children is their father.* **Proverbs 17:6**

One of the greatest characteristics a Godly father can possess is the ability to value one's children. When each child in the family is seen by their father as a precious gift from the King of the Universe, filled with unique potential and possessing a unique destiny assigned to him or her by Creator Yahweh, the responsibility of parenting can become an adventure even in the midst of challenges and hard times.

The little boy placed in your arms the day of his birth will one day be a father and grandfather, just as you are and will be. His destiny is silently pulsing through his very being. Your assignment as His father is to help him discover that destiny and equip him to walk into it. He will need not only skills and education. He will also need to acquire character, good attitudes and a healthy work ethic that will cause him to succeed in the world he will face. He will need to know how to select a life mate and how to love, honor and value his wife and his own children.

Men, I cannot emphasize this strongly enough. Sons can only learn this from their fathers. If you are absent in their lives, they will be left to figure it all out on their own. They will learn from somebody, be it a stranger who does not know God's ways or the television and movie screens presenting twisted images of romance, marriage, and fatherhood. No matter what the culture you live in within our society, you sir, are vitally important in the upbringing of your sons. Any other nonsense told to you is a lie.

Much the same can be said about the little girl placed in your arms on the day of her birth. She will one day be a mother and grandmother. She must know what to look for in a spouse. She must be able to trust a man with her life and the lives of her children. She must know how a Godly man lives his life. She must recognize strong character, good attitudes, and a solid work ethic in another man before she marries him. She must know how a man is to love, honor and value her. She will learn all of this from you. Or she will find what she needs in the life of another man or through the twisted images of manhood, womanhood, and family life she sees on the television or movie screen. Give her the example that she needs and you will save her from a lifetime of heartache and hardships she was never designed and destined to bear. Only you as her father have the potential to help her raise her life's expectations to the high calling of womanhood in God's Kingdom.

Gentlemen, we also need to break down another lie our politically correct culture is trying to make us swallow. The world would have us believe that the single mom is enough for her children. Not true! Mom is not enough for a young boy or young man nor a young girl or young woman. Mom is wired to nurture their lives. You, Dad, are wired to protect, provide and prepare their lives.

I shared this earlier, but it bears repeating again. This image needs to be burned into our minds, men. If we can grasp this, we will better comprehend how important we are to our children. Consider how a woman usually holds an infant. She places the child face toward her, snuggled close to her chest, shoulder or face. A man, on the other hand, holds a child against his chest facing outward toward the world. He holds the child securely so the child has no fear, but in a manner that the child can observe everything going on around them from this very protected state. The infant can learn without fear of being injured.

When the child is older, up on top the shoulders he or she goes. From this position they still feel safe, but are holding themselves upright and able to see and react to what is going on around them with father there to fully support them. Be it a son or daughter, both will feel his gait and sense how he is moving. The experience is not fearful to them. Rather it is one filled with confidence and delight. Mom, on the other hand, will grasp a child's hand to guide them safely to a destination, instructing them along the way and teaching them discernment.

Do you see the difference? It is important that you do. Men, we need to understand that our children will not have a balanced and confident understanding of how to interact with the world around them without our presence in their lives; a presence that makes a significant and meaningful impact in shaping them as strong, prepared, Godly men and women. Mom is not enough. Our children need us.

Our children are a gift from Yahweh. They are also a huge Kingdom responsibility; one that we dare not walk away from. We have no right as men in God's Kingdom to do so. Their potential will be extremely difficult for them to reach without our instruction and support. That, brothers, is a lifelong truth. Even as adults, they will always need their fathers. For a Real Man of God, being an absentee father is not and never will be an option. Embrace your children's lives. You will never regret it.

Our Calling as Fathers

Men, our purpose and destiny with our children is not that much different than what we should be to everyone in our lives. We have a unique and pivotal calling, not only to our own children, but to all in our congregations and in our community. Yahweh can bless, favor and honor a man who jubilantly embraces his role in His Kingdom on earth and go at it with Holy Spirit led passion.

- **Be a leader**. Impart and encourage vision. Help your children discover their own strengths and callings. Give them direction.

- **Be a teacher**. Provide instruction, wisdom, and good counsel. Start with the Word of God as a firm foundation for them to build their lives upon.

- **Be a cultivator**. Provide what is needed to help your children grow in their giftings and skills. Prune when needed. Nourish them at the right times in the right ways. Help them grow healthy and strong emotionally, spiritually, intellectually and physically.

- **Be a protector**. Know when to say "yes' and when to say "no". Be discerning as to when a child is ready to take a risk so that they learn to handle risk well and when they should be kept from a risk altogether. Protect them by teaching them to know what is Godly and what is not. Teach them to value and honor themselves. A healthy self- confidence will protect them from making many foolish mistakes as young adults and beyond. Help them to be able to think for themselves and recognize false teachings and vain philosophies when they see or hear them.

As men we have many roles in life to fulfill. When we grasp that our most important role in all of life is to "build people" by encouraging, exhorting, instructing and empowering them we will have gained a life purpose that will serve us no matter where we live, what we do for an income, or where we worship. Most importantly, we will have gained valuable insight on how to be a better husband and a better father.

Let's Get Practical

We've covered a lot of ground already in this chapter. Hopefully you are inspired and motivated to "go for it" as a father. Yet you and I both know that inspiration and motivation are not enough. We need some practical instruction on how to be all those of good things to our families. Exactly how do we get a firm grip on the steering wheel to keep our children heading in the right direction so that they can arrive at their destinies safe and sound? Let's try to break them down one by one and consider some practical tips.

»*Become the Leader of Your Home*

Leadership begins with you. You must choose to become the leader. You must also grasp that this process sounds easier than it will be. In homes where our wives have been leading (because we didn't have the gumption to do it ourselves) this can be a daunting change; both for us as men and for our wives and children. Though deep down inside, our wives and children might desire the man of the house to lead, making that transition will go against some well ingrained habits. Change is never easy. Before you do anything else, make the choice of becoming a leader before Yahweh and then discuss this choice with your wife. Pray together over this change for your relationship and for your family. Your complete unity as husband and wife in this matter will pave the way for success as, together, you bring this change into your family.

My suggestion then would be to call a "family meeting". As the head of the household, share with your children what you and Mom have been talking about, and allow Mom to communicate to the children that she is 100% in support of this change in your family. Then as a family look at the following Scriptures together. Read them aloud and discuss what they mean and how walking them out might look like in your family. In this "family meeting", fathers, you need to be the one reading these Scriptures aloud and leading the discussion. This may be harder to do for some of you than others, but it will be worth it.

And the LORD said, "Shall I hide from Abraham what I am doing, since Abraham shall surely be a great and mighty nation, and all the nations of the earth shall be blessed in him? For I have known him, in order the he may direct his children and his household after him, that they keep the way of Yahweh, to do righteousness and justice, that Yahweh may bring to Abraham what He has spoken to him." **Genesis 18:17 -19**

You shall love Yahweh your Elohim with all your heart, with all your soul, and with all your strength. And these words which I command you today shall be in your heart. You shall teach them diligently to your children, and shall talk of them when you sit in your house, when you walk by the way, when you lie down, and when you rise up. You shall bind them as a sign on your hand, and they shall be as frontlets between your eyes. You shall write them on the door posts of your home. **Deuteronomy 6:5-9**

Now the days of David drew near that he should die, and he charged Solomon his son saying, "I go the way of all the earth; be strong, therefore, and prove yourself a man. And keep the charge of Yahweh your Elohim: to walk in His ways, to keep His statutes, His commandments, His judgments, and His testimonies, as it is written in the Law of Moses (Torah), that you may prosper in all that you do and wherever you turn." **I Kings 2:1-3**

Train up a child in the way he should go, And when he is old he will not depart from it. **Proverbs 22:6**

Thus says Yahweh, "Stand in the ways and see, And ask for the ancient paths, where the good way is, And walk in it; Then you will find rest for your souls." **Jeremiah 6:16**

Be quick to ask for forgiveness as you identify your failures and express your intention to lead your home much differently from this point forward. Let them know that you are embracing your responsibility as a husband and father to teach them about Yahweh and His ways; that you are not leaving this up to Mom or to the church you attend. Ask for their encouragement, prayer, and support in this change for you and for them. Make them a part of this process. Don't just dump this significant change on them with letting them know what is going on and why.

Also talk about how, as a family of unique individuals, each of you will honor and respect one another as together all of you shift to a different way of managing the household and living in unity. Anticipate questions and challenges along the way. Your entire family dynamic will be shifting. Make time to meet as often as needed to keep the discussion open. Dad and Mom, together you will need create an environment where all family members can feel safe sharing their questions and concerns.

As you can already tell, this is no trivial pursuit on which you are about to embark. This is why I encourage you to talk to Yahweh about this and also discuss this with your wife *before* you bring the children in on it. You will need to make some choices united as husband and wife before you will be able to bring the family together as one in this journey. Have a "game plan". Not all changes are going to happen at once. Choose prayerfully what needs to be taught first, second, third and so forth. Then together you can determine the corresponding changes that will be necessary as your family grows into that new understanding.

Remember, the most effective leadership is leading by example. The changes Yahweh's Word places before your family should be real and meaningful in you first before you dare ask for change in your wife and children.

»Become the Teacher for Your Children

I would suggest teaching your children three very important concepts that will literally change their lives and yours. (You are in this together!) Those three concepts are honor, righteousness and diligence with excellence.

Let me preface these three concepts with the one foundational matter that needs to come first in every human life: a personal relationship with Yeshua the Messiah. Everything else you and your family build must rest upon that chief cornerstone. Without Him, all your efforts will be vain and simply "religious". You will have a great looking life but there will be no "life" in your spirits or souls.

There isn't a single human being on the face of the earth that can truly live out the ways of Yahweh perfectly. There is no human soul without sin ("missing the mark" that His Word sets before us to live by). Yeshua's death on the cross, burial, and resurrection is the only way that we can stand before our Creator and King fully forgiven in our shortcomings.

Accepting Yeshua as my Messiah means that I know it is He that saves me from my failures and shortcomings. I confess my sin to Him and ask for His forgiveness. It is through Him that I have right standing before my Creator, fully delivered from having to live as the world around me lives. I am restored to life in His Kingdom on earth as life was intended for all mankind in the very beginning. I am fully able to learn to live on earth as it is in heaven.

When we settle our "sin and failure issues" with Him, the King of the Universe then fills us with His Holy (unique, uncommon) Spirit placing within us seeds of all His best characteristics: love, joy, peace, patience, kindness, goodness, faithfulness, gentleness, and self-control. We are empowered to live out His ways without the weight of our guilt or shame. Our former passion and desire to do as we please, gives way to a new passion and desire to do what pleases Him, our King. In fact, we begin to delight in living as He has instructed us! Those seeds of His character begin to sprout and grow. We begin to become more like Him.

Men, when you are walking in this Kingdom truth for yourself and have a passionate relationship with the Messiah, this becomes the first and most important life step you can lead your children through as their father. You as their loving father can teach them all about honor, right living and diligence with excellence based upon Yahweh's Word but without having their own vibrant relationship with the King, they will never fully understand why these things are to be so very important to them and to the world in which we live. They will live without the big picture of all that Yahweh is doing in this world. Even more tragic, they will miss out on grasping a personal understanding of their role and destiny in that big picture.

The absolute best gift you can ever give your children is to introduce then to our Messiah and walk with them as they build their own unique relationship with Him.

Honor

Honor is the key message of the Torah (God's Teachings and Instruction). Choosing to honor Yahweh's instructions will bring blessings and favor into the lives of your children and your grandchildren. Choosing to dishonor Yahweh's instructions will bring curses and disfavor into the lives of your children and grandchildren. Blessings and favor cover every area of our lives: financial, physical, emotional and spiritual. (Read Deuteronomy 28 – 30.) Yahweh is a King and a king is bound by his word, both to the blessings he proclaims and to the curses he proclaims. This is exactly why Yahweh is so very clear in His Word concerning what is honorable to Him and what is not. He desires for us to walk in His blessings and favor but that choice remains ours.

The Hebrew people have understood this for thousands of years. When we and our children choose to honor His Ways, things go well for us. When we do not, we bring disaster upon ourselves. The solid Hebrew father believes what Yahweh said about His blessings and curses resting on the following generations. The Biblical principle is called "The Law of Merit". Every sinful (dishonorable) act will reap its consequences to the third and fourth generations. (Exodus 34:7) Every righteous (honorable) act will reap its blessings to the 1000th generation! (Deuteronomy 7:9) Simply by choosing to repent and change to a lifestyle of honoring Yahweh's Teachings and Instructions will literally change the direction of your family's future generations. When we honor His ways we will always succeed; even in the direst of circumstances or under the severest of testing and trials.

What and who should we teach our children to honor? How about starting with the basics, which couldn't be spelled out much more simply than in the Ten Commandments. There are four great "honors" in in the Ten Commandments (called the "Ten Words of YHVH" by the Hebrew people).

The first great honor to teach our children to practice is to honor Yahweh, Creator and King of the Universe. What that looks like is spelled out in the first 4 commandments:

- ☐ Recognize and embrace Yahweh as your Deliverer, the source of your Salvation.

☐ Do not allow anything or anyone to become "a god" in your life. Give Him first place in all of your activities, worship, and relationships.

☐ Do not bow down to worship anything that is created by Yahweh or by man. Worship only the Creator, who is Yahweh.

☐ Do not take His name in vain, meaning never take Him, His Word or His lifestyle lightly or attempt to improperly use His Name, His Word, or His lifestyle. Do not ignore or belittle Him.

The second great honor to teach our children to practice is to honor Yahweh's Shabbat (the Sabbath). Notice I said Yahweh's Shabbat, not man's Christian tradition. We are to follow the same pattern and cycle of rest He established in His universe at the very beginning of its creation. Contrary to popular teaching and belief in most churches, in Yahweh's Word (Old Testament and New) this has never changed. Man, through Roman Emperor Constantine, changed it in 325 AD in an effort to assimilate Christians into pagan ways and thus completely ostracize *both* the Jews and any follower of Yeshua that continued to practice "Jewish" Sabbaths and Feast Days.

Choosing to honor Yahweh's Shabbat on the seventh day of the week then instructing our children to do the same is pleasing to Him. It will also do wonders for your wife and your children. Why? Because it is a time of speaking blessings based on Yahweh's Word over each member of our families. Their self-confidence and sense of personal purpose will sky rocket, thus assuring them that as they continue in Creator's ways, a path of prosperity is theirs to walk out and enjoy.

The third great honor to teach our children is to honor their father and mother. This instruction from Yahweh has an incredible promise for those who walk in it. *"...that your days may be long upon the earth."* Teaching a child how to honor a person – especially a parent – once again begins with you, Dad. Your child will learn how to honor Mom by watching how you honor her. The same applies to Moms. You child will learn how to honor Dad by watching how Mom honors Dad.

Men, your sons have a great lesson to learn from you in this area. Hebrew men have understood for centuries that when a man honors his wife things go well for him both inside and outside the home. They will learn how to do this as you bless your wife each Shabbat with the beautiful words of Proverbs 31 that you meaningfully speak to her. They will learn to honor Mom and someday their own wives as they see you opening doors for her, helping her with heavy tasks around the house, supporting her talents and dreams, providing for her needs, protecting her from all harm, and listening to her opinions and ideas without criticism.

Your children will also learn how to honor Dad and Mom as they watch both of their parents honor their own parents. Do you call or visit them regularly? Do you go to greet them the moment they enter the room? Are they the first people you greet when you enter their home? How do you speak about your parents in the presence of your children? Have you taught them by your example that honor is due a parent regardless of whether you agree with them on matters or no matter how poorly they may have treated you as a child or adult?

Our culture is missing a key understanding of honor, especially in regards to parents. Honor is not something that is earned. It is something that is given. Your wife's parents need to be honored simply because they raised their infant girl into the marvelous woman who now graces your life. They did not do it perfectly. You may not agree with them on all things or even get along with them.

Regardless, your wife would not be in your life without them nor would your children. Honor them. Teach your children to honor them. (Wives – in regards to your in-laws, the same principle applies to you.)

The fourth great honor to teach our children is to honor all human beings. This too is found in the Ten Commandments. Honor the very life of a human. Do not murder (take an innocent life). Honor the deep relationship of your marriage covenant with your spouse, nor cause another to dishonor their marriage covenant with their spouse. Do not commit adultery. Honor the hard work of others. Do not steal their belongings (including their ideas). Be truthful and honoring in your words about another human being. Do not bear false witness against a neighbor. This means no slander, no half-truths, no outright lies, no gossip. Honor the success of others. Don't wish you had their wealth, possessions, servants, cars, boats, televisions, hot tubs, etc. Don't be trying to connive ways to get them to give anything to you or manipulate your way into their world so you can enjoy their stuff. Have pure motives and be genuine in your relationships.

When asked which of the commandments, was the greatest Yeshua answered, *"You shall love Yahweh your God with all your heart, with all your soul, and with all your mind. This is the first and great commandment. And the second is like it: You shall love your neighbor as yourself. On these two commandments hang all the Law [Torah] and the Prophets."* **Matthew 22:35-40**

Love without honor is not true love. Love does not allow us to dishonor anyone. Honor is pivotal to our King. If we are to walk in His understanding of love, we must teach ourselves and our children to honor.

Righteousness

This is a loaded word in Christian circles. We are absolutely correct in our understanding that our righteousness is the righteousness of our Messiah. He clothes us in His righteousness as we stand before our Creator and it is only in Him that we can claim that righteousness. It is not of ourselves.

Yet His covering of righteousness over us does not give us license to live just any old way that we want to. He still expects us to be able to know the difference between right and wrong, holy and unholy, clean and unclean. If we do not know these things, how are we to rule and reign on the earth standing with Him as His Bride upon His return? Where is this kind of Kingdom discernment found? It is found in the Torah.

Teaching our children to live out Yeshua's righteousness in our own lives is critical to their safety and well-being in this world and in preparing for their role in the new world that He will usher in. The apostles teach us that we are to walk and live as He did upon this earth.

Yeshua was most definitely compassionate, kind and gentle. Yet He spared no harsh words against hypocrites and the self-righteous. He called them out for their falsehoods and twisted understandings of His Word. He tore down their manmade traditions and taught the people to return to the purity and Spirit of God that purposely exists within the Torah. He called them back into His Kingdom lifestyle and back to their destiny as a nation of His priests and kings upon the earth.

He did not call them into legalism. As fathers, we need to grow in our own understanding of what it means to keep His commandments out of a heart of passion and love for our Messiah. Yeshua said, "If you love me, obey my commandments." (John 14:15) The Torah is the commands of Yeshua. He and the Father are One. Yeshua is not going to contradict or go against the Word of Father given at Mt Sinai. He said,

> *Do not think that I have come to abolish [destroy, do away with] the Torah or the Prophets. I did not come to destroy but to fulfill [bring full understanding]. For assuredly I say to you, till heaven and earth pass away, one jot or one tittle will by no means pass from the law [Torah] until all [the Prophets] is fulfilled.*
> **Matthew 5: 17-18**

Look out your window, men. Is heaven and earth still there? Has all that the Prophets wrote of come to pass? Guess the Torah is still here for us to learn from then, isn't it. In fact, John tells us in both his gospels that Yeshua and the Torah [Word of God] are one in the same.

> *In the beginning was the Word, and the Word was with God, and the Word was God and the Word became flesh and dwelt among us.* **John 1:1-14**

It is the Word of God, the Torah, birthed out of the very Spirit of God and made flesh in the person of Yeshua our Messiah that instructs us on what the King of the Universe considers right from wrong, holy from unholy and clean from unclean in His Kingdom.

Men, teach your children the Word of God! His Word teaches us the lifestyle of His Kingdom, which separates all of His children from the traditions, religions and systems of the world that we live in. Our children will not live successfully in their divine destiny as priests and kings of His Kingdom on earth if they are not taught His Kingdom and its ways. They will celebrate feasts that have nothing to do with His Kingdom. They will eat foods that are not to be eaten in His Kingdom. They will worship on the Sabbath of Roman and Greek gods rather than on the Sabbath of their King. They will not know right from wrong and honor from dishonor. The consequences of that lack of knowledge will bring death to their jobs, businesses, homes, relationships and even their own physical bodies. That is how the King designed it and decreed it. He will be faithful to His Word, both the blessings and the curses.

Choosing to walk in the Ways of His Kingdom is not about legalistic observance of the Torah to try to earn our own righteousness. Our salvation and right standing with Father comes only through His grace poured out to us through Yeshua our Messiah. The choice to walk in His Kingdom is about our love toward Him and its heartfelt expression in simple obedience to the teachings and instructions (commands) of the One who makes us righteous through His own great sacrifice. John put it well when he penned.

> *He who says "I know Him" 'and does not keep His commandments, is a liar, and the truth is not in him. But whoever keeps His word, truly the love of God is perfected in him. By this we know that we are in Him. He who says he abides in Him ought himself also to walk just as He walked.* **I John 2: 4-6**

What is my first suggestion in teaching your children to walk in righteousness? Once again, start with Yeshua's Sabbath, sundown Friday evening to sundown Saturday evening. Lead your family in this change. Learn together the powerful richness and beauty that is found in stepping into the times and season of His Kingdom. I promise you, in this one small act of obedience, your walk with Yeshua will become more than you ever imagined it could!

»Teach Diligence with Excellence

How do I say this nicely? I am not sure that I can, so here goes. People are becoming increasingly lazy with each generation. I battle it myself and so do my wife and children. Granted, since the turn of the last century, the pace of life is in many ways much faster and more pressured. However, I don't think that it is my imagination when I state that the general work ethic in today's society is lacking.

We have become "entitlement minded". "I deserve this and that" rather than "how can I work to make this happen for me and my family?" We have unions to tell us how long to work and how hard. We have peer pressure that does the same. But what does the Bible teach us about work ethic?

> *He who has a slack hand becomes poor, but the hand of the diligent makes rich.* **Proverbs 10:4**

> *The hand of the diligent will rule, but the lazy man will be put to forced labor.* **Proverbs 12:24**

> *For even when we were with you, we gave you this command: if someone won't work, he shouldn't eat! We hear that some of you are leading a life of idleness not busy working, just busybodies! We command such people and in union with the Lord Yeshua the Messiah we urge them to settle down, get to work, and earn their own living.* **2 Thessalonians 3:10-12**

Men, teaching our children that their potential will only be discovered and released through getting out there, trying their hand at things and working to develop their knowledge, skills, and talents is one of the greatest gifts a father can give a child. It is your wife's role to nurture your children. It is your role to teach them how to succeed in the world around them.

Watch your children as they grow. Look for their talents and interests to manifest. What talent or skill makes them stand out from those around them? That is the key to their success! Guide them in pursuing excellence and never giving up on becoming the best that they can become at what they enjoy and causes them to stand out from all the rest.

When they fail in an attempt at something, teach them how to get back up, dust themselves off, and keep trying. If what they are trying to do just isn't working, don't criticize or put them down. Instead, help them find a better fitted interest or skill pursue. Teach them how to shine and to help others to shine, too.

Be sure your children have basic life skills to successfully manage life and also to help others. Do they know how to use common tools around the house and yard? Can they change a flat tire? Do they know how to keep up routine maintenance on a vehicle? Can they balance a checkbook? Do they know how to plan and budget their expenses? Have they ever mowed the lawn or taken care of infants and younger children? Do they know how to cook a nutritious meal (applies to both girls and boys)? Do they know how to shop wisely? Can they wash their own clothes? These are essential skills responsible adults need. Teach them now, before they leave home. Don't be afraid to start young; just be sure to gauge their learning to their age.

As your children enter their teen years, do they know how to save and invest for their future? If they are going to pursue a trade, help them find the best place to get training. If they are going to pursue a career or start a business, help them find they best place to further their education. Do they know how to honor and respect their employer? Have they been taught to take initiative and to problem solve? Can they readily identify a need and develop a way to meet that need? Are they able to set goals, write them down, and develop a plan to achieve their goals? Do they understand how banking, insurance and investing works, and how to protect their assets as they acquire them? Have they been taught to tithe to Yahweh? Have they been taught to give of their time and their resources to charities and those in need?

»Teach Your Children that Prosperity is in Them

It is your job as a father to help your child learn to draw out from within them the ability to prosper and confidently run with it. They will not find what they need to prosper by playing video games or watching TV and movies hours on end. Get them out of that false world and teach them to interact with the real world as much as possible and according to Yahweh's principles and instructions, of course. Here are a few other tips that I have given to other fathers and have found helpful myself.

- Clearly write down all instructions of anything that you are expecting of your children. This includes chores, house rules, curfews, etc. Make your expectations understandable so that there is no room for confusion or doubt. Help them succeed!

- Never confuse a child's identity with a punishment. Be sure they know it is a poor choice of action or inaction that they are being disciplined for, not for who they are.

- Teach your children that there are consequences to sin. Choices to go against Yahweh's wisdom and instruction will result in things not going well. Dishonoring God and others will bring painful situations into one's life. Children need to know and understand this.

- Teach children the true meaning of repentance and how to repent. To repent is much more than saying "I am sorry". True repentance is owning up to an mistake or poor choice, saying "I am sorry", making good on any loss to the person you have wronged, and then choosing never to do that again. Teach them also how to receive forgiveness and move on. Do not let them dwell in guilt or shame. Teach them to readily forgive others and never hold a grudge.

- Teach children the power of sowing and reaping not only financially, but also in deeds, words, choices and attitudes.

- Teach children that a successful and happy life is about pursuing excellence, not perfection. Mistakes and failures are bad only when we fail to learn from them and keep trying.

▢ Teach children to be leaders, even when they are following. There is always opportunity to lead, even if it is the family dog. Leadership requires taking responsibility. The best leaders are those who know how to serve others, even while they are leading.

▢ Teach your sons how to love Yahweh, a spouse, children, their neighbors. (Women seem to have how to love down pretty well; men need help in this area!)

▢ Teach your children to have standards and convictions based on God's Word and on a personal relationship with Him. "If you don't stand for something, you will fall for anything." Let them see you praying, reading the Word of God, obeying His instructions and commands, seeking to follow Him in a personal relationship, worshipping Him with all your heart and standing for His truth. Create a hunger in them to have the same. Discuss His Word with them and teach them how to find His answers to their questions.

▢ Teach them to enjoy work. Yahweh created us to work, to multiply and to prosper in every area of our life. Work is not a curse. The struggles and things that try to destroy our work (the thorns and thistles) are the curse. Work is meant to bring joy and fulfillment as we build His Kingdom upon the earth.

Men, fatherhood is the most rewarding responsibility a man can have. Yahweh is our Father and He loves every moment of the experience. We should too.

I want to leave you with one last thought in this chapter. If we as adults living in this declining world are being challenged and put through trials and tests that often threaten to overwhelm us, how much more are our children dealing with now? How much more will they have to deal with as adults? Don't make the mistake of thinking that their childhood somehow makes them immune to the wrongs and evils that are in this world.

As adults, all of must not become so consumed with our own problems that we can't take a moment to look into the eyes of our children and see the turmoil that is bubbling inside of them, especially in our teenagers. Our churches are dying and our children are being swept away in the world's vain philosophies and religions, often simply because we are not paying attention and not fulfilling our responsibility to them. It is time to turn this disaster around.

Fathers, it is time for us to take courage and be true fathers. It's time to take our selfish eyes off of ourselves, our pleasures and comforts and help this generation that we have brought into this world. We must, for the sake of our King and His Kingdom, look into the hearts of our young people, into the very souls that will make up this world's future and extend our hands to help them. If we who call ourselves by His Name do not, someone else will.

I tell my son this all of the time. Any fool can father a baby. Only a Real Man of Yahweh can be a tremendous father. How about you? Are you up to the challenge?

Chapter Six:
Becoming a Faithful Steward

Gentlemen, we now come to that area in our lives that has to do with our finances. There is so much confusion in church teachings about money and wealth. If you have a church background that has involved multiple denominations or TV preachers, you have heard everything from poverty vows to tantalizing prosperity teaching. As is usual, the Truth from God's Word is far more balanced than either of these extremes.

Money is not a bad thing, but the love of money is. Having wealth is a good thing, but being greedy and coveting is not. Working for increase is a healthy pursuit, but working yourself to death merely for material gain is not. The truth is that we need money and financial wisdom to live in this world. Believe it or not, God created wealth to begin with. To Him it is a good thing. It is the attitude we take and the way we use wealth that is of utmost concern to Him. Yes – once again, it is an issue of our hearts toward Him and toward those He places in our lives along the way.

Yeshua spoke a great deal about wealth and riches in His time with us. In fact, this topic is one of the most often mentioned topics in all of Scripture. Why? Yeshua said it best. "Where your treasure is reveals to God and to others where your heart really is." (My paraphrase.) This is why Yahweh addresses this topic from Genesis through Revelation. Wealth is a needed resource and a tool. Wealth is also His blessing for those who loyally live in His Kingdom. He delights in the prosperity of His servants! Key words: His servants. He knows that He can joyfully entrust His wealth on earth to those who in loving obedience wholeheartedly serve Him. However, we are never to become obsessed with wealth or allow it to cloud our judgement.

Adam was not poor. Neither was Noah. (It took a lot of wealth to build that big boat!) Abraham and Isaac were the wealthiest people in Ca'anan. Jacob was wealthy. David started as a shepherd boy and became a wealthy King over a wealthy kingdom. Solomon was the wealthiest man ever...and the wisest...until he strayed from God's Word. Then his sons and grandsons lost it all. Historically, the Jewish people following the Biblical financial principles found in God's Word have prospered no matter where they have been scattered. This remains true to this day. This begs a question. If we are grafted into Israel through Messiah Yeshua, why are we not prospering? Perhaps it is because we lack Biblical knowledge, understanding and vision regarding handling finances, wealth and business. Men, it is time to change this!

I could write a whole book, probably several books, on Biblical wealth. There are a number of good books out there already and I encourage you to read them. I recommend authors like Dave Ramsey, Larry Burkett, Bob Harrison, and Dave Williams. For right now, however, I want to cover some of the basic financial concepts and a few tidbits of wisdom to help you get your mind growing and your financial feet moving under you.

Why care about money and wealth?

Money and wealth are crucial to three major parties in your life. First, money and wealth are important to Yahweh and His Kingdom on the earth. Second, they are important to your own completeness and well-being. Third, they are important to your wife, children, and children's children. How you choose to approach and handle money and wealth reveals your heart to all three...and it greatly affects how you positively or negatively impact all three. In essence, next to the number one issue regarding the quality of your relationships with

God and people, your thoughts and actions concerning money and wealth come in a very close second.

In **Matthew 25:14-30**, Yeshua shared a parable about wealth that is often used for all sorts of spiritual applications. For our purposes in this chapter we are simply going to look at it at face value. As you read, think about this teaching in the context of Yahweh, His Kingdom, and you. Which servant (or steward) are you in regards to money and wealth?

> *"For it [the Kingdom of heaven at the end of days] will be like a man about to leave home for awhile, who entrusted his possessions to his servants. To one he gave five talents [equivalent to a hundred years' wages]; to another, two talents; and to another, one talent — to each according to his ability. Then he left.*
>
> *The one who had received five talents immediately went out, invested it and earned another five.*
>
> *Similarly, the one given two earned another two. But the one given one talent went off, dug a hole in the ground and hid his master's money. After a long time, the master of those servants returned to settle accounts with them.*
>
> *The one who had received five talents came forward bringing the other five and said, 'Sir, you gave me five talents; here, I have made five more.' His master said to him, 'Excellent! You are a good and trustworthy servant. You have been faithful with a small amount, so I will put you in charge of a large amount. Come and join in your master's happiness!'*
>
> *Also the one who had received two came forward and said, 'Sir, you gave me two talents; here, I have made two more.' His master said to him, 'Excellent! You are a good and trustworthy servant. You have been faithful with a small amount, so I will put*

you in charge of a large amount. Come and join in your master's happiness!'

Now the one who had received one talent came forward and said, 'I knew you were a hard man. You harvest where you didn't plant and gather where you didn't sow seed. I was afraid, so I went and hid your talent in the ground. Here! Take what belongs to you!'

'You wicked, lazy servant!' said his master, 'So you knew, did you, that I harvest where I haven't planted? And that I gather where I didn't sow seed? Then you should have deposited my money with the bankers, so that when I returned, I would at least have gotten back interest with my capital! Take the talent from him and give it to the one who has ten.

For everyone who has something will be given more, so that he will have more than enough; but from anyone who has nothing, even what he does have will be taken away. As for this worthless servant, throw him out in the dark, where people will wail and grind their teeth!'"

Men, what has Yahweh placed in your hands? In His temporary absence, what of finances and wealth has He entrusted to you to create increase for Him and for His Kingdom? Is it possible that upon His return Yeshua will hold us accountable for what we did or did not do with the money and wealth that He has provided for us? I believe this is, at face value, exactly what Yeshua is driving at. To understand this we need to embrace our calling as men upon this earth that belongs to Him.

At creation, all was as Yahweh intended and mankind was in charge. We were to be His rulers upon the earth, under His Divine Sovereignty and in accordance to His instruction and decrees. At the fall of mankind, along with our relationship to Him a perfect world become broken. Since that time, through His many covenants with mankind and with Israel, His goal has been to deliver us and restore to us that ability to repair this broken world. We do this by sharing the good news of His Kingdom – that it is indeed possible to enter again into that Kingdom through Yeshua and begin to set the world back on track. We do this by restoring His sovereignty in our lives and the lives of our families. We return to His Ways.

Men, it takes money and wealth – Biblical wealth – to repair what is broken on this earth. Take a good look around. Our families are broken. Our communities are broken. Our host cultures are broken. The nations of this earth are broken. We must remember that first and foremost, through Messiah, we are Israel. Most of us live in host cultures such as the USA, Europe, Asia, South and North America, Australia, Africa, and the Middle East. Each of these have 100's of imported subcultures and indigenous peoples. In YHVH's sight, ALL of these cultures are broken.

We have been commissioned by Messiah to take the good news into all nations, all cultures, and make disciples. We are to walk with those who respond to our Messiah and make Him their King too. We are to teach them His Ways and thus restore the broken world to His Kingdom. We have an enormous mission to accomplish. We need the people of His Kingdom to prosper in every way, including in money and wealth. Remember those historical men (and women) I mentioned earlier. There were "culture changers"! They knew who they were and they lived not only to have a good life, but to make a difference. Like us, they are given the choice to make a positive or negative impact. Like us, they will be held accountable.

Before we go any further, let's define a couple of key concepts already brought up. First, we need to understand what Biblical wealth is. Then we need to understand what it means to be a servant or steward of that wealth on His earth.

Biblical Wealth

Biblical wealth is measured financially by three assets: precious metals, land, and livestock. A truly wealthy man holds all three. Historically, precious metals eventually became the first currency. Coins of general circulation were made of precious metals. (Amazingly, this remained true in many nations and cultures until the 1960's. Today you have to make a special purchase to get coins made of precious metals.) Land was once mostly agricultural. For land to truly be valuable it had to have a good source of water. Today land is called real estate: agricultural, residential, and commercial. Livestock consisted of animals of high value to that culture that could be used for agricultural and transportation purposes. Livestock also meant you had the means to feed your family, because these animals were used to farm the land or slaughtered for food. In some regions of the world, the ancient values of holding precious metals, land and livestock still hold true. In modernized cultures, it is important for us to know what holds lasting and true value where we live. We also need to be mindful that as the days on this earth become more difficult before Messiah returns, the original assets of Biblical wealth are going to become increasingly important again.

Biblical wealth is also measured by the size of a man's family and the Torah-based wholeness of his family relationships. A man is considered to be wealthy when he has acquired a good and Godly wife with whom he has a healthy, loving, and prosperous relationship. His wealth is then increased by his children and grandchildren – again with whom he has healthy relationships and has effectively taught and led them in God's Ways. (This kind of wealth is what the first five chapters in this book were designed to help you accomplish.) Godly friends are also considered to be a true blessing from YHVH and worth a great deal of "relationship wealth" in our lives. A man who walks closely with YHVH may not have a large number of close friends; however, such friends who have chosen and are able to walk with such a man are worth their weight in gold!

The Faithful Servant or Steward

"Steward" is a days-gone-by term that we seldom use today. Yet, because we operate in a Kingdom of YHVH mindset, to us it should be a very relevant term. The Merriam-Webster dictionary defines a steward as "one employed in a large household or estate to manage domestic concerns (such as the supervision of servants, collection of rents, and keeping of accounts); a fiscal agent." Likewise, Merriam-Webster further defines stewardship as "the conducting, supervising, or managing of something – especially the careful and responsible management of something entrusted to one's care". Perhaps the best modern term for "steward" is "manager". We are the faithful managers of the things of Yahweh's Kingdom here on the earth.

As men of YHVH's Kingdom, we are entrusted by Him to manage so much. By covenant we are entrusted to be good managers of the land, the sky, the waters and all that these contain. We are to be good managers of God's Word – guarding, protecting, living by and teaching it to our children and grandchildren. Yeshua then reminds us that we are to be good managers of every provision and increase that Father places under our care. Wow. To be good managers, good servants of our King, we certainly do need His instruction, wisdom and guidance. Men, we also need to pray for and encourage each other. We need to seek out Godly instruction and learn from those who have succeeded before us. In regards to finances and wealth, we most certainly need a good, firm foundation.

Financial Wisdom from the Word of God

The best tool we can use to build a firm financial foundation is God's Word. The "condensed version" of God's wisdom in regards to money and wealth is the Book of Proverbs. I encourage every man (and woman) to read a chapter from Proverbs every day. There are 31 chapters, so on our Western calendar that works out really well. Highlight or underline every verse that addresses wisdom, wealth, money, giving, lending, and greed. Over time, these sound principles will settle deep into your heart and mind, giving you tremendous direction in times when financial questions come before you. In our world, financial decisions usually come in two forms: wise opportunities for Godly increase or unwise temptations that become your financial downfall. The principles found in Solomon's Proverbs will help you to know the difference.

Your financial future, and the financial future of your family for generations to come, depends on what you choose to do with money from this day forward. Men who recognize the importance of becoming the man YHVH has destined them to become are diligent about developing a good work ethic and using sound financial principles…and they are diligent about passing these Kingdom attributes on to their children.

THE BIG PICTURE

A good man leaves an inheritance to his children's children, But the wealth of the sinner is stored up for the righteous. **Proverbs 13:22**

Financial independence is something we all desire for ourselves and for our children. Most of us were not born with wealthy parents or relatives to leave us a rich financial inheritance. A good number of us may have grown up in underprivileged conditions. The good news is that our financial future does not depend upon these scenarios! In the verse above, Solomon instructs us that a good man – a righteous man following God's Ways – leaves an inheritance to his children and his grandchildren. Notice that he doesn't say "thinks about" or "probably should" leave an inheritance. He says this as a foregone conclusion. If you are living a righteous life according to God's

Word, you will do this. Creating an inheritance becomes a part of your life vision and mission. You make plans to succeed and become financially independent...and you act on those plans.

You may be asking, "Just what is financial independence?" In a nut shell, financial independence looks like this:

- You are completely out of debt.
- You have created enough passive monthly income that you no longer have to work a job or be self-employed to meet your needs. (This is accomplished through saving, having a wise investment plan, and often building a business.)
- As God directs...you can live where you want to live, in the house you want to live in, drive the vehicle you want to drive – all without debt.
- You can give generously, building the Kingdom and meeting needs in your community.
- Your time is fully yours to delegate to the purposes Yahweh gives to you.
- You are able teach your children how to do what you have done.
- You are able to leave a wealthy inheritance to your children and grandchildren.

Wouldn't this lifestyle be awesome? I'm not there yet. But I am heading that way! You can too. You start by simply making a choice and dedicating yourself to embracing God's financial counsel, changing your money habits, and take action.

I also like the second part **Proverbs 13:22**. "*The wealth of the sinner (those who live outside the Torah) is stored up for the righteous (those who live by the Torah).*" Now, I have heard a thousand sermons teaching that this is a prophetic End Times promise that somehow the wealth of the world is going to miraculously transfer into the hands of believers in Messiah. This may be true and I would gladly receive it. But this is not the face value teaching here. Solomon is telling us that the wealth of the sinner is built upon folly and greed. This person and his descendants are destined to lose that wealth…and the wise righteous man will benefit from what the unrighteous have lost. In other words, by using God's financial wisdom, we become able to gain and keep for our children and grandchildren what the unrighteous lose. Men, opportunity is knocking all around us! It's time to embrace God's financial wisdom and learn how to harvest what the ungodly wealthy unwittingly lose every day.

As we prepare to look at some practical steps in creating a sound financial future for you and your family, pause for a few moments and ask yourself "Why"? The stronger your "why" the stronger your determination and efforts will be in achieving the picture you have for your family. Your ability to succeed at the goals you are ready to make will be driven by the strength of your "why". Your "why" may be similar or quite different than your friend's "why". That doesn't matter. Your "why" will become the passion that fuels you and makes the diligence and work worth it. Maybe your "why" is simply because you want to better fund the ministries involved in building God's Kingdom on the earth. Maybe your "why" is that you refuse to allow a generational pattern of poverty go any further in your family line. Maybe you have seen the tragedy of close family members who live their final years in financial distress and unmet medical needs. You have simply determined that you and your wife deserve to live your later years in comfort and security. Whatever you reason, your "why" is a critical part of your financial success from this day forward. Know what it is and clearly write it down somewhere where you will see it every time you face a financial decision.

Now you are ready to start setting goals for your financial well-being and wealth building. Keep them realistic yet lofty enough to keep you challenged and inspired. Create a picture in your mind of what a financially free life will look like for you. Better yet, start a "dream journal" and write down what you believe Yahweh is showing you is possible for your life, not just financially but in the career path He has given you, family goals and dreams, etc. Listen to His heart for you. Remember, He delights in blessing His children! I personally like to go through magazines and cut out photos that depict what Father has shown is His heart for me. I glue them into my Dream Journal. When I get discouraged or find that I am losing my focus, I get out my Dream Journal and prayerfully start paging through. It usually doesn't take much time before Yahweh has my heart and mind encouraged and I can move forward again.

Assuming responsibility for your finances and the financial future of your generations takes effort yet is so very worth it. You and your spouse will need to get honest with how you, united as one, are handling money. Together you will need to identify where you both need to unite in your priorities and improve financial skills. Questions you will want to answer together will include: How much does it cost us to live each month? Do we need to find creative ways to bring in a more consistent or larger income? What are our giving goals? How much do we need to save for emergencies? How do we plan for expenses that come around annually or quarterly? Do we want to start a business in the next few years? What will that take? As you answer these types of questions you will be empowered to set realistic goals that will guide you in creating a plan that you can follow month by month to achieve those goals. In this initial process, you and your spouse might feel overwhelmed by what you discover. Take a deep breath and remember that anybody can eat an elephant, one bite at a time.

Now that your "why" and your initial goals are established, the work of sowing, diligence, and reaping needed to achieve your financial goals begins. It's time to take a hard, honest look at your lifestyle.

Are you spending money on "wants" or "needs"? Learn to discern the difference. It is okay to spend on what you truly need, and far wiser to save money toward what you want. Do you have bad habits that are costing you a fortune? Do you need to adjust some priorities?

For instance, I have a city friend that absolutely had to have a four wheel drive pickup truck decked to the max. He was spending a small fortune on truck payments and fuel. Truthfully, he really didn't need that truck. He wanted that truck. It made him look and feel rough and tough. It fed his ego! When he came to his financial senses, he sold the truck and bought a good car (with cash, not a loan) that had great fuel mileage. It didn't take long before he realized that he had an extra $1000 a month in his hands simply because he adjusted his priorities, tempered his ego, and got rid of that truck. That money got put to work as he paid off his other debts. He now places all those additional funds into his savings and investment funds. He is singing a whole new happy tune!

It is sometimes hard to stay on track with your goals and following a budget. Saying "no" to all those wants that beg to be bought is not easy. But it is worth it – VERY worth it. You are not in this fight for financial success alone! Your Father Yahweh is right there with you…and your spouse and family, once they see the big picture and feel the benefits, will be right there with you too.

KINGDOM FINANCIAL PRINCIPLES

1. **Work…with honor and excellence!**
   Men, work is not a curse. Work is a blessing. Even Adam had God-assigned work to accomplish before sin and toil entered the earth. Doing the work YHVH destined to you to do is actually enjoyable and rewarding. Working with honor and excellence leads to obtaining a good reputation and opens the door to opportunities that often go beyond what you dared to dream

possible. Working with the simple purposes of honoring YHVH, caring for your family, and providing a service that meet the needs of others is the higher path on which God's Word instructs us to walk. If you have been reluctant work, today is the day to change your mind and your habit. We all want the perfect job doing exactly what we want to do. But if that is not available to you at this moment in time, don't use that as an excuse to do nothing. Work is essential to providing well-being for your family and in building a foundation for your financial prosperity. When it comes to working, that old motto, "if life throws you lemons, make lemonade" is so very, very true. Righteously do what you have to do to create earnings and increase. Proverbs 10:4, Proverbs 14:23, Proverbs 18:9, Proverbs 20:26, Proverbs 21:25, Proverbs 22:20…and the list goes on!

2. **Steward His Increase…Manage the Money!**
   Yes – it is that ugly word: Budget. If you are like me, you don't like the word "budget" because use of a budget comes loaded with concepts like constraint and discipline. Yep. True. If the word "budget" sounds oppressive, use other terms that visually reveals another truth - you are now in charge of your financial destiny. Call it "Our Financial Management Plan", "Our Spending Plan" or "Our Kingdom Budget". The name isn't important. The principle is! A budget puts you in charge of your money rather than your money in charge of you. You will always have the knowledge of exactly where you are financially so that you can plan and maneuver your funds as you need to, when you need to. You will discover that there are ways to reach the end of the month not broke. Stick diligently to this building step for those first three months and don't give up on making this tool work for you. I promise you, you will start to see savings accumulate and those surprise expenses become far less painful. Budgeting makes you "the Boss" of your hard earned dollars.

You will never want to live without one again.
Proverbs 11:14, Proverbs 27:23-27

Creating a budget is a team effort. Be sure you are both included in the planning. Guys, if she best at creating the budget, let her do it. Then go over it TOGETHER each month, make adjustments, and come to an agreement that this is the plan for the next 30-31 days. If you are the "budget nerd", the same applies in reverse. A couple of encouraging words about marriage in regards to budgeting. Men, by using a budget your marriage will be in far less strife. You have a plan. Each of you has agreed upon what is going to be spent, saved, and invested. All the fog and indecision you may have known before is removed. All the fear created by not knowing exactly where you are financially is gone. Both of you can handle the household funds with confidence at all times. In truth, you have just released a new sense of freedom in your home. The dark, oppressive cloud of financial fear and indecision is gone. Believe me, the results will bless and improve your marriage!

Creating a budget means adjusting and setting your priorities. Are you spending money on things you really don't need? Do you have bad money habits that are costing you a fortune? The old saying of "pay me now or pay me even more later" is absolutely true. With compound interest added to credit purchases you really will pay later!! Get a handle on your spending by writing down what you spend money on. You might be surprised out how much of it flies out the window with seemingly insignificant choices. A little sacrifice of some of those habits now will bring great blessings of enjoyment later. Remember – it is not what you make that is important. IT IS WHAT YOU SAVE and how you put that money to work for you that will determine your lifestyle at your retirement.

Think you won't need a budget when you become wealthy? Wrong! Wise, wealthy people still have budgets. Those who don't go broke fast. Athletes and celebrities are often prime examples of this downfall. Think about this. A successful business or a large corporation lives or dies by the effectiveness of their budget and their ability to function by it. Do we seriously think we can do less for our own families and households? In many ways our households are businesses – the facility needs to be managed, the personnel given instruction and cared for, daily tasks assigned to a team committed to a family vision…and the finances need to be budgeted so that they are appropriated wisely. You and your wife are the CEO's and the CFO's of your family!

3. **Learn to be a Multiplier**

    Mankind was created to multiply. This directive from YHVH is not only about having children and grandchildren. This directive applies to everything we as humans put our hands to. We were not created to be satisfied with stagnation or decrease. We were created in His image – and He is all about creativity, growth, prosperity and increase. We are to creatively grow our households, farms, ranches, businesses, employment skills, and financial and property holdings. We follow God's Ways (the Torah) so that we will have the favor and blessing of YHVH to prosper (increase) in everything we do. The following principles will set you up for multiplication…and serve as the perfect guide to "how to create a Kingdom Budget"!

    ♦ **Tithe and Offerings.** FIRST THINGS FIRST - give to Yahweh what is HIS. The importance of putting this principle into action is enormous. The tithe – 10% of your earnings and increase - sits at the top spot in your budget at all times and in all circumstances. The tithe goes to the

House of YHVH that serves your relationship with YHVH and is there for your family in good times and in bad.

Offerings are given during the Feast Days to honor YHVH and to aid the poor, widows, orphans, and to crisis needs. These are "voluntary" in that the amount is between you and YHVH. You give an offering according to what He places on your heart to give. The Feast Days are the Sabbath, the New Moon each month (Rosh Chodesh), Passover, Feast of Unleavened Bread, Day of First Fruits, Pentecost, Day of the Trumpets, Day of Atonement, and Feast of Tabernacles.

According to God's Principles and Instructions (the Torah) the tithe and the offerings are not optional actions. These are His instruction given to His good stewards until He returns. Obediently following them comes with His promise of abundant provision and overflowing blessings.

Over my years in ministry, I've learned that the first issue to address with folks who come to me in financial hardship is the issue of tithes and offerings. I am serious, men. If you are not tithing (10% of your earnings and increase) do not expect to be blessed. If you are not presenting offerings above the tithe during the seasons of His Feast Days, your blessings will be limited.

I have seen it over and over again. Once those in hardship trust Him with His instruction and adjust their mindset and action in regards to tithing and offerings, their finances begin to turn around. Promotions at work take place. New and better job opportunities suddenly surface. Needs seem to get miraculously met, simply because they repositioned themselves according to God's instruction. Many discover that by putting Yahweh first with that 10% tithe they start living better with the 90% than when they, out of desperation, kept it all and refused to give. The Kingdom principle is simple. Because of their decision to walk in obedience, the King is now free to bless and show favor. We must remember that we are in covenant with Him, and He keeps His word – both the blessings and the curses equally apply. Our choices and our actions affect what He can and cannot do for us.

♦ **Tzedakah.** Giving is truly a matter of the heart. Yahweh tells us that He loves a cheerful giver. When was the last time you gave to meet a need just for the pure joy of being able to give? I'm not talking about the tithe or the Feast Days offerings. I am talking about giving in addition to tithes and offerings. In other words, giving to meet a human need. In Hebrew this kind of giving is called tzedakah… an act of righteousness that is just and meets our covenant obligation to help others. This kind of giving isn't always "giving out of my abundance". It may require a sacrifice…the giving up of something that might even be precious to me. This kind of giving often doesn't make any rational sense to others, or even to me. It is, however, in obedience to a unique and special instruction Father has spoken to the heart by His Spirit. His instruction might be to meet a person's financial need, like a one-time gift or monthly support to a missionary family, paying a month's rent for someone who has lost a job, or helping to pay a medical bill. Maybe its meeting a physical need such as groceries, filling a gas tank, or even giving a car or house to someone in need. It might even be less personal – like donating to food banks and homeless shelters. The one common thread is "meeting a human need".

I like to call this "radical giving" because it usually radically tests my relationship with my Father. Do I honestly believe and trust in His love for me so much that I am confident that cheerfully giving what He is asking of me will not harm me? In helping meet another's need, do I truly believe He will meet my needs too? This is radical love in action … and once you start giving radically you start down a path of increasing trust and confidence in Yahweh only a handful of us ever choose to experience. The joy found in meeting needs through cheerful giving is indescribable!

4. **Pay yourself first.**
   After you give your tithe and offerings to YHVH, pay yourself first. This means before any bills or demands on your money are paid. Remember even a small amount of money saved over time will yield a good rate of return. Start with an Emergency Fund with a minimum of $1000 for emergencies (car repair, appliance break down, etc). Make this a priority. This will prevent needing to use a credit card for an urgent issue. If you use any of that $1000 it needs to be replaced ASAP. Later, after your debts are paid off, build that Emergency Fund into 3-6 months of living expenses and place in a money market savings account so that it will earn interest and be accessible to meet your needs in a true emergency.

   Make "pay yourself first" the priority. If at the start of the month it looks like there is not enough money to pay yourself first and still make it to the end of the month, determine what needs to be cut out. Keep "needs" – like food, housing, transportation, and insurance. Cut "wants" – like eating out, going to the movies, and even cable or satellite television. In the long run, believe me, you will not regret sticking to this priority.
   Proverbs 11:14

5. **Get out of Debt ASAP (and stay out of debt!)**
   Once you have met that initial $1000 Emergency Fund, get aggressive towards all debt. Your house mortgage is fine for now, as long as you are not living in home that is beyond your financial means. The rest of your debts need to be paid off as quickly as possible. When they're paid off you can tackle paying off the mortgage early. (If you don't have a mortgage, don't get

one until all of your other debts are paid off. And never go beyond a 15 year pay off plan with firm intent to pay even that off early.)

Men, debt does not honor YHVH, nor does it bring honor to you or your household. Sometimes debt such as medical debt cannot be avoided. However, if you are "paying yourself first" most debt can be completely avoided and emergency debt can be paid off quickly. Debt is slavery to a world system called "compound interest" and it literally cripples, if not completely destroys, your financial potential and your family relationships. Proverbs 22:7

6. **Become a Smart Investor.**
    By the time you reach this step you should be on a roll! You have a finely tuned budget, 3-6 months in your emergency fund, and your debts paid off. You are ready to do some serious investing – and you now have the funds freed up to do so. I highly suggest you meet with a financial planner or wealth manager to set your investment goals according to your household's specific scenario. Those of you in your 20's and 30's will need a far different investment plan than those in their 40's, 50' and 60's. Those of you who are married with children need a far different investment plan than young couple without children or empty-nesters.

    Be diligent in your search for professional help in making and carrying out your investment plans. Work only with those who understand and live by the same Biblical financial principles that you now do. I would suggest contacting organizations like the Dave Ramsey Financial Peace University to ask for referrals for financial planners or wealth managers in your location. Once you find someone who is the right fit for you, let them instruct and mentor you on how to become a smart investor…and never agree to do something with your money that you do not understand and feel comfortable with.

Understand the Power of the Compound Interest System

Men, we live in a "have it now, pay for it" later culture…and, boy, do we pay for it later. Credit cards, school loans, personal loans from friends and family, home equity loans, and so on are eating up our financial foundations like a swarm of termites. Our houses are literally in risk of collapsing around us. Debt is damaging our marriage relationships and hurting the destiny of our children. I'm as guilty of allowing credit to become my master just as much as anyone else. (There's a reason it's called MasterCard!) Debt in this compound interest world can rob me of having funds to reach my financial potential and puts a huge roadblock in the path of my career potential. I am sick and tired of living in like this. Are you?

The truth is, compound interest is the eighth wonder of the world. He who understands it EARNS it. He who doesn't, PAYS it.

The banking and credit industries are like any other business. They are out to make a profit. Interest on secured and unsecured debts is their biggest money maker. They literally spend more money – in the billions each year - on marketing credit card services and loans than any other product they offer. And we fall for it over and over again. (Ever wonder why they hand out those tasty little suckers at a bank?) They understand compound interest and have created a way to make billions of dollars with it. They use compound interest to EARN by getting those who don't understand it to PAY them.

It's time for a little educational eye-opener. Do you understand how the compound interest system in the credit and loan industry is working AGAINST YOU? Here's an example. It's a Sunday afternoon and football season is over. The wife and you are out shopping at the mall and as you walk through the department store you find yourselves in the furniture department. The two of you start chatting about how badly you need to replace that sofa you bought at a garage sale 3 years ago. There it is…the perfect size and color for your living room. It's a nice sofa and the wife absolutely loves it. A salesperson shows up and points out that it's on sale for $3000. If you buy it today you will save $500! Out comes the credit card. That lovely sofa goes home with you and you are thrilled that you saved so much money by buying it today.

Hold on a minute! Let's look at what really just happened. You made a sofa purchase of $3,000.00 at 18% interest, deciding like most that you can "handle" the monthly minimum payment. Brother, with the compound interest on this "loan" it will take you 10 years to pay off that lovely sofa at an additional cost of over $2,002.00 in interest. Yep. You just bought yourself a $3500 sofa "on sale" for $5002.00. Some bargain that was – and it probably won't even last those 10 years. Gentlemen, it is time to get off this train ride heading you towards a financial wreck. Stop buying into this vicious system. Stop PAYING compound interest. Cut up the credit cards NOW!

Choose to Make Compound Interest Work FOR You

Once you are debt free you are ready to flip things around and, like the banks and credit industries, learn to use the compound interest system FOR you by investing. When you make investments you want the highest compound interest rate possible. Here is an example of what happens with a lump sum investment made by you, the investor, over time. (Maybe you can't start with a lump sum of $10,000…but do work toward starting with something!)

Initial Investment = $10,000

Time	Rate of Growth					
(Years)	5%	6%	10%	11%	15%	20%
5	12,763	13,382	16,105	16,851	20,114	24,883
10	16,289	17,908	25,937	28,394	40,456	61,917
15	20,789	23,966	41,772	47,846	81,371	154,070
20	26,533	32,071	67,275	80,623	163,665	383,376
25	33,864	42,919	108,347	135,855	329,190	953,962
30	43,219	57,435	174,494	228,923	662,118	2,373,763
35	55,160	76,861	281,024	385,749	1,331,755	5,906,682
40	70,400	102,857	452,593	650,009	2,678,635	14,697,716

Now let's look at how a monthly investment of only $250 with a good compound rate of interest will work FOR you over 25 years. Wow! Men, the younger you start and the more that you can invest month by month, the more you will make.

Wealth Accumulation after 25 Years, Inflation-Adjusted

Monthly Investment	Annual Rate of Return										
	4%	5%	6%	7%	8%	9%	10%	11%	12%	13%	14%
$ 3,500.00	$1.23M	$1.39M	$1.58M	$1.80M	$2.06M	$2.36M	$2.71M	$3.13M	$3.61M	$4.18M	$4.85M
$ 3,250.00	$1.14M	$1.29M	$1.46M	$1.67M	$1.91M	$2.19M	$2.52M	$2.90M	$3.35M	$3.88M	$4.50M
$ 3,000.00	$1.05M	$1.19M	$1.35M	$1.54M	$1.76M	$2.02M	$2.33M	$2.68M	$3.09M	$3.58M	$4.16M
$ 2,750.00	$963k	$1.09M	$1.24M	$1.41M	$1.62M	$1.85M	$2.13M	$2.46M	$2.84M	$3.28M	$3.80M
$ 2,500.00	$876k	$992k	$1.13M	$1.29M	$1.47M	$1.69M	$1.94M	$2.23M	$2.58M	$2.97M	$3.46M
$ 2,250.00	$788k	$893k	$1.01M	$1.16M	$1.32M	$1.52M	$1.74M	$2.01M	$2.32M	$2.69M	$3.12M
$ 2,000.00	$701k	$793k	$902k	$1.03M	$1.17M	$1.35M	$1.55M	$1.79M	$2.06M	$2.39M	$2.77M
$ 1,750.00	$613k	$694k	$789k	$899k	$1.03M	$1.18M	$1.36M	$1.56M	$1.80M	$2.09M	$2.42M
$ 1,500.00	$525k	$595k	$676k	$771k	$882k	$1.01M	$1.16M	$1.34M	$1.55M	$1.79M	$2.08M
$ 1,250.00	$438k	$496k	$564k	$642k	$735k	$843k	$969k	$1.12M	$1.29M	$1.49M	$1.73M
$ 1,000.00	$350k	$397k	$451k	$514k	$588k	$674k	$775k	$893k	$1.03M	$1.19M	$1.38M
$ 750.00	$263k	$298k	$338k	$385k	$441k	$506k	$581k	$670k	$774k	$896k	$1.04M
$ 500.00	$175k	$198k	$225k	$257k	$294k	$337k	$388k	$447k	$516k	$597k	$693k
$ 250.00	$88k	$99k	$113k	$128k	$147k	$169k	$194k	$223k	$258k	$299k	$346k

There is absolutely no reason on earth why a 25 year old man who is debt free and chooses to invest on a monthly basis can't become a millionaire by age 50 simply by making compound interest work FOR him. The higher the interest rate, the better he will do!

How to Pay off Debts

Now that you understand the power of compound interest, are you a little more motivated to get rid of your debt ASAP and start investing? You should be! The skill you need now is how to pay off that debt as quickly as possible.

My hat is off to people at Dave Ramsey's Financial Peace University and the folks at a company called Primerica. These dedicated individuals have helped millions of people – including myself – learn how to get out of debt. Both teach a system that is called "debt stacking". Ramsey calls it "The Debt Snowball". Men, IT WORKS. Not only does your debt begin to quickly disappear, but you will also literally save tens of thousands of dollars in interest. This will be your money that, by using that power of compound interest, you will put to work for you. Men, if you are serious about saving your family's financial future and becoming a man who knows how to steward the wealth of God's Kingdom, you will commit to aggressively attack your debts using this system. (Remember to tuck away that initial $1000 in your Emergency Fund before you start your "debt stacking" payoff plan.)

Instructions and an Example

1. List your debts smallest to largest. Add them together for your total debt payoff amount.
2. Beside each debt list your minimum payment amount on that debt.
3. Now, go through your monthly budget and cut wherever possible. Then take that amount and add it to the minimum payment on that smallest debt at the top of your list. This is your new monthly payment on that debt until is paid off. (Keep your other minimum payments the same.)

4. When that first debt is paid off, roll that payment amount on to the next debt on your list. By adding the payment amount to the minimum payment on the next you will discover that it too will pay off much more quickly. Keep at it with that new amount until that debt is paid off.

5. As soon as the second debt on the list is paid, do the same with the next debt on your list. Using the same approach as step 4, keep adding to those minimum payments as you move down your list. Repeat until you are debt free!

EXAMPLE:

Credit card #1	$1500.00	Minimum Payment:	$25.00
Credit card #2	$2200.00	Minimum Payment:	$35.00
Credit card #3	$3200.00	Minimum Payment:	$42.00
Car loan	<u>$16,124.00</u>	Minimum Payment:	$325.00
	Total $23,024.00		

1. After going through the budget you have come up with $275 you can add to paying off debts.

2. Add that $275 to the $25 minimum payment on Credit Card #1 until that bill is gone.

3. Now you have $300 to add to the payoff efforts on Credit Card #2. Your monthly payment will now be $335 until this debt is paid off.

4. Moving on down the list, you now add that $335 to add to the monthly payment on Credit Card #3. Your new payment is $377. When that debt is paid off, roll that payment amount to the next debt.

5. Next is the Car Loan. Your new payment will become $702 till the day that Car Loan is paid off. When that last payment is made, you are DEBT FREE.

6. THE NEXT STEP? Take that $702 a month and give your "Pay Yourself First" plan a healthy raise! Or apply the $702 to your mortgage payment and get your house paid off!

Men, I cannot emphasis this enough. ACT NOW to get rid of your debts! If you do it now, you will be even further behind ten years from now. Remember, you are where you are today because of what you did last year, five years ago, even ten years ago. Don't keep doing things the same old way with your money. You are better than that!

A Final Financial Nugget

Brothers, I trust that you see by now that the biggest hindrance towards your financial independence is YOU. The mindset you choose to have in learning and applying wisdom in managing the money and other increases that YHVH places in your hands will be what determines how well you will achieve the lifestyle you want and fulfill the destiny YHVH has placed in your heart. There is an amazing amount of literature and videos available out there along with counselors that pledge to help you. Some will provide sound advice based on God's word. Others will not. Choose who you listen to very carefully. Acquiring and practicing Godly wisdom and instruction will empower you to reach your goals of becoming wealthy and change the financial picture of your family line forever. Following ungodly counsel and instructions will hinder your financial future at every move.

I'm not saying that there is nothing to learn from the ungodly. There are business skills and concepts that they have become experts at in areas like starting a business and making stock market and real estate investments. Learn those skills…but do not follow any counsel that they give that goes against God's Word. Be wise by grasping on to what is worth learning and tossing away the rest. Be patient and choose to live and do business only according to YHVH's Kingdom principles. YHVH will bless His good stewards!

Chapter Seven:
Becoming His Disciple

The highest calling a man can choose to accept is the call to become Yeshua's disciple. To do so will forever change the way you walk as a man, as a husband and as a father. To answer His invitation to "come and follow me" sets your path for an incredible journey in the challenge of being the man God purposed and created you to be. But, before anyone accepts this call of discipleship, you need to understand what you are getting yourself into. What does it mean to be a disciple? How do we as men live and walk in that kind of relationship with our King?

I've discovered that in our Western culture, we as Christians (followers of Christ) are caught up in a struggle that most don't even realize exists. It is a struggle between two very different mindsets. It is also this struggle that causes a tremendous amount of confusion and conflict in the church and in synagogues also, for that matter. One mindset is Greek/Roman and developed out of centuries of paganism from the Tower of Babel till now. The other is a Hebrew mindset that flows directly from the image and character of our Creator, revealed to us in the Hebrew language in the Hebrew Scriptures, recorded and preserved for us by a people group chosen and called out by Him to be His light in a dark world: the Hebrew.

Since the 4th century AD, the church has adapted its doctrines and the meanings and applications of the Scriptures to conform to the Greek/Roman culture, language and lifestyle that still permeate our Western society today. Yet our Savior and Deliverer was promised to come and came through the Hebrew people, language, and their scripture-based culture and lifestyle. Yahweh was making a statement! The Savior of the world could come only through a people that honored and preserved His ways because the ways of the King never change and they never will.

Yeshua was thoroughly Hebrew and He still is. So were His 12 disciples, the apostles and a majority of the first century church. Their lifestyle, mindset and application of Biblical teaching and instruction were ardently consistent with the Hebrew Scriptures, which we now call the Old Testament. They did not see themselves as new or different than their ancestors. Their only mark of "being different" from other Jews was their belief that Yeshua, a Jewish rabbi and descendant of King David, was and is the promised Messiah of Israel. The only thing "new" was that Messiah, the Master Teacher was revealing to them a far greater depth and purpose to His ways than they had ever understood before! Gone were man's traditions and misinterpretations. Everything about the Torah, Prophets, and Writings (Tanakh/Old Testament) seemed new and fresh again. Even more amazing, now this incredible Truth was fully empowered by the presence of God's Spirit dwelling in and with them day by day. They could now confidently the walk that God had always intended for them. His Kingdom had come fully into their lives in mind blowing living color and authority!

Men, before we move on, you need to understand something very significant as we begin to explore the call to be Yeshua's disciple. It concerns our English Bibles and the Greek-based meanings of the key words they contain. Translations are never as good as the original. The use of the common language of the day to offer a teaching based on another culture and mindset will fall far more flat than if it was expressed in the native language of the speaker or writer. For example, I can use the German language to a German audience to express a strongly American concept but I can guarantee you that it will not come across the same as it would have if I said it in American English to an American. Even English words used in America carry a far different meaning in jolly old England.

Paul, when writing in Greek, faced the same issue. He could use Greek words in his speaking and writings, but the meanings of the Hebrew concepts he was attempting to teach were sometimes "lost in translation". Paul was an extremely intelligent person who was a master at both languages, yet the translation problem still hampered his efforts. This is exactly why Peter said that many of Paul's teaching are difficult to understand because unless you are well taught and stable in your knowledge of Hebrew Scripture and application, they can be twisted so far off it can destroy the Truth in you. (2 Peter 3:14-16) Brothers, this is the state of the modern Western church.

However, the opposite is also true: if you know and understood the meanings of the Hebrew idioms and concepts that Paul often shared using Greek words of his day then the understanding you gain is powerfully life altering! His educated Hebrew audience (in Rome, Galatia, Ephesus, Corinth, etc.) understood the true meaning of His teachings, but much was and still is completely lost to everyone else. This is certainly true all the more so today.

I say all of this because I want you to grasp that what we often think is "being a disciple" falls very short of what a Hebrew in the time of Yeshua understood as discipleship. Bear with me! This is so vitally important. I would not try to explain it to you if it wasn't.

What Is A Disciple?

"Disciple" is the English word translated from the Greek word "mathates". It simply means "learner, pupil, student". When we hear these words today, we think of sitting in a classroom or a church pew and listening to a teacher instruct us on just about anything from math to philosophy to an inspirational message. If we like the lesson well enough we just might actually try to apply it in our everyday life. If not, no big deal; the choice is fully ours. Being a student is a matter of our own choice. We can choose to show up for class or not show up at all. We can also absorb a tremendous head full of knowledge that we can easily regurgitate, but never allow it to truly change our lives. In fact, we can even become experts in arguing the facts or opposing ideas, yet still live pretty much as we choose. The relationship is pretty much based on the intellectual transfer of information and adherence to the belief system of the teacher (at least enough to get through that final exam).

Not so in Hebrew discipleship. The word "disciple" in Hebrew is "talmid". It also means "student, disciple" in English. However, in Yeshua's time and still today, the meaning goes much deeper. The Hebrew root word for talmid is "tamid" and it means "eternal light". As Yeshua's disciple, my destiny is to become an eternal light to this world, just as He is. My goal is to become like Him in every way: character, thinking, actions, belief system and lifestyle. His "Eternal Light" is to become the essence of my own existence. For me, that is a huge transformation from where I was to what I have become and to what I will become as He continues to transform my understanding. I have true hope that I can be transformed into His likeness. The wonderful part about this transformation is that it does not happen by my efforts only! I am constantly being transformed "not by might nor by power, but by My Spirit." That is the promise Yahweh found in Zechariah 4:6. Plus I have the promise of Yeshua that He is always with me!

Just as important as becoming eternal light is the second Hebrew meaning found in the word "talmid" (disciple). That meaning is "to be a student of the Torah". It is Hebrew understanding that one cannot become "eternal light" to others without studying the Torah. For followers of Yeshua who understand that He is the Living Torah in the flesh, this has a powerful dual meaning. As His disciples, this means we must study to know His Word – the Tanakh (Genesis to

Malachi) - and we must also study to conform to His character and Kingdom lifestyle. Our goal is to correctly understand Yeshua's life and teachings on the Torah as He dwelt upon the earth (Matthew to Revelation) and fully adapt to Him. As the Book of Revelation tells us, those found in His Eternal Kingdom at the end of time are ones who keep both the commandments of the Father (found in the Torah) and the faith of Yeshua. (Revelation 14:12) We must be able to sing both the Song of Moses (the Torah) and the Song of the Lamb (the life & teachings of Yeshua). (Revelation 15:3)

Let's consider another hugely significant difference found in the Hebrew concept of discipleship. Remember that I stated earlier that in the Greek mindset the choice to become a disciple is purely my choice, dependent upon what I want for myself. That implies that once "in the Rabbi's circle", I have the option of doing whatever I want with what I am being shown and taught. However, in Biblical Hebrew culture, a man does not choose to become the student of a Rabbi (which means "teacher"). The Rabbi chooses the student. I cannot "invite myself"; I must be invited. If I accept the call of the Rabbi, I then become responsible to act upon all that I learn. His invitation is crucial because the dynamic of true discipleship is far too intense for a Rabbi to take a risk on just anybody.

The Rabbi fully intends to walk in a very close and powerful relationship with His talmid. Not only will there be a transfer of knowledge and information. There will be a mentoring process going on 24/7. There is one goal in this relationship and one goal only. The disciple is to become like his Rabbi. He will eat the same foods, say the same prayers, wear the same type of clothing, worship as the Rabbi worships, speak the same language, and transform his lifestyle to that of the Rabbi. He must become exactly like his Rabbi in every way, including in character and nature. The success of this transformation lies completely in 1) the strength and commitment of the relationship between the Rabbi and his student and 2) a relationship with Yahweh that allows His power to be at work in the life of the disciple. Both relationships are based on tremendous trust. Discipleship is not meant for the faint of heart. It takes courage.

The Rabbi chooses his talmidim (disciples) carefully. He looks for men (and women) who have the right heart and the right attitude. He knows who has what it will take and who does not. He does not take on a student just because the man requested to be one. The man is chosen and called. Do all of the Rabbi's choices succeed? No, some fail. But the Rabbi knows that failure will be by the student's own choice, not because they don't have it in them to succeed. He chooses them based on the potential he recognizes in them. The choice to reach that potential is theirs to make.

The Rabbi knows that it will take time, energy, patience and grace to mentor his students at such an intense level. Everything he says and does with his talmidim have a purpose and meaning that will not change at any time in the future. He is equipping them for life in God's Kingdom. What he teaches them must become an irreversible part of their lives when he is with them and when he is not. The Rabbi is fully aware that his time with them is far too precious to waste. He knows head knowledge alone will never be enough for them to succeed. The truths of the Instructions and Teachings of Yahweh must reach their hearts and change their lives. A good Rabbi will not waste his time on teaching the trivial, nor are his teachings "subject to change" when his time with them is complete. He goes to the heart of every matter with His disciples. They are expected to respond not only in words, but in a change of character and daily life. "Pew warming" is not allowed.

Frankly, men, this Hebrew understanding of being a disciple can come across as intimidating. But it should be like that! Men, don't we deeply long for and want to be challenged like this? With the Hebrew understanding above, let's look at what happened with Yeshua's disciples and I think you will see what I mean.

And as He walked by the Sea of Galilee, He saw Simon and Andrew his brother casting a net into the sea; for they were fishermen. Then Yeshua said to them, "Follow Me and I will make you become fishers of men." They immediately left their nets and followed Him. When He had gone a little father from there, He saw James the son of Zebedee, and John his brother, who were in the boat mending their nets. And immediately He called them, and they left their father, Zebedee in the boat with the hired servants and went after him. **Mark 1:16 – 20**

Were these fishermen new to Yeshua? No. He had seen them before. Remember, He had been teaching in northern Galilee for a while by now. These men were Jews. They belonged to the local synagogue, had been raised under a rabbi's teaching, had studied and memorized Scriptures as children and gone through their Bar Mitzvah's. These rough and tumble men in the family fishing business had heard Yeshua speak more than once and seen His miracles already. Their presence in the crowds that listened to Yeshua revealed one thing; they had hearts for the Truth of God's Word and His Kingdom that Yeshua was teaching. They deeply liked what they were hearing from Yeshua as a Rabbi. They were drawn to His nature and character. They wanted more and Yeshua, a master Rabbi who was astounding the experts with His teaching, knew it.

So one bright sunny day while the guys were about their everyday business, Yeshua walks by and sees them busy at their trade, just doing life as they usually did. Yet, He sees far more than that. He sees their hungry hearts and He sees their potential as men of His Kingdom. They look up from their work and see Him approaching. Can you imagine what is going on in their mind and emotions? "Why is He coming toward us? What will He say? How should I respond? Could it be? No, I couldn't possibly be worthy of that honor! I am just a smelly fisherman! Maybe He simply needs to buy some fish. Yes, I am sure that's it."

Then the thing they dare to dream possible happens! Yeshua, the Master Rabbi everyone in the region is clamoring over, says to them, "Follow me! I am going to make you just like me – a fisher of men's souls and lives." He gives them the call and invitation of their craziest dreams! "Come and be my talmidim!"

With absolutely no hesitation, these four men drop what they are doing and walk away. Andrew and John leave their father sitting in the boat! From their Hebrew perspective, they would be fools not to. This is not an everyday occurrence in the life of every man in Judea. A Master Rabbi had called them. This was HUGE! Their hearts were hearing "You have what it takes to become just like Me." Think about this in regards to all of the twelve; a bunch of fisherman, a tax collector and other ordinary hard working men. They had a common education, common skills and common lives. There was nothing special or elite about them, except for their heart for the things of Yahweh and His Kingdom. In this matter, they were unique and filled with tremendous potential! Yeshua spoke to their potential and they responded "Yes!"

Men, Yeshua is still calling men out to become like Him. The potential He placed in them before they were even born is to become men of His Kingdom on this earth. He is calling us out, men. The time is now – NOW like it has never been before. Our once Scripture-based culture and lifestyle is crumbling all around us. Our children are lost; lost to the truths of a grace-filled and loving God who has given us instructions on how to live and prosper, lost to a hope for their futures and a majority lost to the stability God has designed in the treasure of a secure, stable family life. Men, WE are the answer to this tragic dilemma. You and me.

Maybe we should be asking ourselves, "What is the cost of NOT becoming His disciple?" Our families, our communities and our nation; they are the cost. This is a price that I, as a husband and a father, am not willing to pay. To truly be like Him in every way flies in the face of our collapsing culture. Being His disciple, in the truest meaning of the word may cost me my job, my current comfortable location, a few close friends or family members who do not understand, and other things as well. There is a cost to becoming like Rabbi Yeshua, my Messiah, but the cost not to be like Him is even higher.

I am reminded of a point in Yeshua's relationship with the Twelve of his many disciples. Yes, many chose to follow Him, but only 12 were of HIS choosing. The passage is found in John 6:60-66, where upon hearing a very difficult teaching given by Yeshua, many of the crowds of "disciples" left him.

> *From this time on, many of his talmidim [disciples] turned back and no longer traveled with him. So Yeshua said to the Twelve, "Don't you want to leave too?"*
>
> *Shim'on Kefa [Peter] answered him, "Lord, to whom would we go? You have the word of eternal life. We have trusted, and we know that you are the Holy One of God."*

Peter understood his commitment, as did the other of the Twelve. They had left everything and they knew who He was. For them, there was no place else and no one else they would want to turn to. They could not and would not turn back, despite what the crowds thought. That, gentlemen, is courage.

In my own life, I have heard the King's call to me to be His Kingdom Man upon the earth. How awesome it is to know that He is saying to me, "Steve, you have what it takes! Walk with Me and let Me change your life. Let me show you how to be My eternal light in this world." I have said "Yes!" Will you?

Remember, John told us that Yeshua is God's Word (The Torah, the Prophets, and the Writings – the Tanakh) made flesh to live among us and teach us His ways. Yeshua existed with God before Genesis and He is God. John understood. He got the revelation so many are lacking today. It was Yeshua who made the world and everything in it. It was Yeshua who gave the Torah to Moses so the people of His choosing (He has always been a Rabbi!) could become His Eternal Light to the nations. He invested 3.5 years of life on earth re-instructing those He had chosen at Mt Sinai on the correct understanding and lifestyle of His own Words. This same Yeshua died to atone for the failures all who would choose to respond and call Him Messiah, Lord and King. He made us clean again, free from our failures - past, present, and future. Not just so we can be saved from hell but also so that we could learn how to live like He instructed us to. He gave us His very own Spirit, His Breath, to empower us to learn the ways of His Kingdom and live in them with joy, delight, and blessings. His Spirit comes to us to write the words of His Covenant on hearts that are no longer stone and minds that are no longer bound by deception.

That, my brothers, is Eternal Light! This is the Good News! The greatest hope that we can offer this dark, hurting world is His Kingdom - on earth as it is in heaven. You are CALLED TO BE MEN of His choosing; ready to willingly adapting to His ways. You have the potential to become Eternal Light to your spouse, your family, your business, your community, your nation and the entire world. Your destiny as a man of God and His Kingdom is to go out there and help others become that same Eternal Light, starting with your own household! Will you step up to take on the challenge the Master Rabbi has called you to?

Go therefore and make disciples [eternal lights, students of the Torah] of all the nations, baptizing [immersing] them in the name [character and lifestyle] of the Father and of the Son and of the Holy Spirit, and teaching them to observe all things that I have commanded you [He is King]; and lo, I am with you always, even to the end of the age. **Matthew 28:19**

How to Start Being His Disciple

Brother, if you have chosen to keep reading, I am assuming Yeshua has already begun to stir up that Eternal Light burning within you. You are seriously considering responding to His call to become His disciple. Now the first of many choices ahead is yours to make.

The first question before you is the same question Yeshua posed to His first disciples. Yes, you are joining with them. They were His first. There have been many since. You are next in line.

> *When Yeshua came into the region of Caesarea Philippi, he asked His disciples, saying, "Who do men say that I, the Son of Man, am?"*
>
> *So they said, "Some say John the Baptist, some Elijah, and others Jeremiah or one of the prophets."*
>
> *He said to them, "But who do you say that I am?"*
>
> *Simon Peter answered and said, "You are the Messiah, the Son of the living Elohim [God, the I AM]."*
>
> *Yeshua answered and said to him, "Blessed are you, Simon Bar-Jonah, for flesh and blood has not revealed this to you, but My Father who is in heaven."* **Matthew 16:13-17**

Brothers, Yeshua asks the same question of each of us today. "Who do *you* say that I am?" Your answer to this question is the beginning of the walk that will change your life. If you are not sure of this answer in your own mind and heart, this is where you must start. Who is Yeshua? Scripture tells us that He is God, the Word of God, the King of Heaven and of Earth, Creator of all things on earth, Creator of mankind and the promised Messiah of Yahweh's covenant with His people, Israel. Messiah's very name, Yeshua, means "Yahweh is Salvation/Deliverance". Is Yeshua all of this to you?

If not, then your immediate need is to simply ask the Father to give you revelation regarding who Yeshua truly is. Many who call themselves Christians (or Jews) still need greater revelation on this matter, so don't feel bad if you are personally unsure. Just know that if you are sensing Yeshua calling you to be His disciple, this is the first question you must settle for yourself. It is a good thing that He is asking you, "Who do you say that I am?" This means you already have tremendous potential within in you!

The question of Yeshua's identity is the key issue for all of his disciples. If He is merely a great teacher, another prophet, a good and Godly man or just another divinity among many other gods to choose from, then you have declared yourself "free to choose" regarding His instruction to you. You can discard any one of His teachings or instructions based on what you think of them. His Torah (His instruction and teaching) becomes optional. You believe you have the authority to pick and choose what suits you. In fact, you can do away with the Torah entirely because you believe they are merely old words not relevant to who you think He is. In essence, you have decided that your thoughts are greater and hold more authority than His.

However, if Yeshua truly is God, the Word of God, Creator and King of the entire universe and all it contains, the promised Hebrew Messiah who has come to get all mankind back on track and living in His Kingdom, that revelation changes everything. If Yeshua truly is making us His priests and kings to rule with Him on the earth someday and He is the High Priest and Great King over His priests and kings...guess what? *His Word – the Torah - is the final word.* This is a Kingdom we are living in, not a republic or a democracy. We adapt to our Divine King so that we become like Him in His nature, character, and lifestyle. He does not adapt to us, nor is He subject to our opinions, traditions, or doctrines. His instruction and teachings are to be followed. They are not suggestions. They are not for us to pick and choose. Most importantly – *they are for our benefit!*

He, as our good Father and King, gives us the perfect path to a blessed and favored life that is filled with joy, peace, and prosperity. In fact, He delights in being able to bless and favor His people for they have become both citizens of His Kingdom and His very own children. Life in His Kingdom is meant to be abundant and amazing! But, He has to be the Divine and Supreme King, not just another god among gods.

Divinity or Divine? A god among many gods or the Almighty God? A king among many kings or the Supreme King over all? Good man or Messiah? *Yeshua is asking you, "Who do you say that I am?"* The nature of your future, both in this life and in eternity, rests on your answer.

When Yeshua becomes your King and your High Priest, every instruction, decree and teaching found throughout the entire Bible, not just the New Testament is understood to come directly from His throne. Yeshua did not and will not change His Word. He did come to correct our understanding and confront us on what we have made of His Word. He is still doing the same today.

Yeshua constantly challenges us as His disciples, "Did I say that? Or did a man, or the great deceiver, say that? Do you do that because I said to, or because your traditions and doctrines have made it so? Did I set the timing of the Sabbath or do you follow what a tradition or decree of a man says it is? Did I establish the Holy Days forever or do you abandon them and follow what a doctrine or a man say they should be? Did I establish what justice and morality are to be, on earth as it is in heaven – or do you conform to the ways a culture or society say they should be?" Did I say you could dishonor and mistreat your parents, spouse and children and get away with it without serious consequences? Why are you not conforming to Me, your King? If you really love Me as your Father and as your King, you would keep my commandments. You would stop dishonoring

Me with your words and actions. What did I, your King and Almighty God, say?"

Men, rest assured that Yeshua's challenging questions are always wrapped in immeasurable love and amazing grace! He wants His absolute best for us in every area of our lives. Yet, He is bound by His Word as our King. He can only bless those who love Him with all that they are and have, and love others in the same manner as they want to be loved themselves. He spells out what that looks like first in His Word, and then in the very life He lived as He dwelled with us on earth. He is the same yesterday, today, and forever. Wise is anyone who chooses to respond "yes" to the call to be His disciple. Wise is the man who chooses to say "yes" to His call to be true men of His Kingdom!

As we approach the return of the Messiah, an enormous battle is intensifying. This shouldn't surprise us because the battle over the earth and the hearts of mankind is not new. It is battle between two kingdoms: the Kingdom of Darkness being run by the Prince of Darkness, Lucifer and the Kingdom of Light which is under the full sovereignty of the King of the Universe, YHVH (Yahweh).

Through the prophet Zechariah, Yahweh tells us, *"Because of the blood of your covenant [with Me]...I declare that I will restore double to you. For I have bent Judah, my bow [the Jews], fitted the bow with Ephraim [the 10 lost tribes and foreign pagans that have returned to His Ways], and raised up your sons, O Zion, against your sons, O Greece, and made you like the sword of a mighty man."* (Zechariah 9:13) The lifestyles and philosophies of man through all of the past and present cultures and kingdoms of this world - Egyptian, Babylonian, Persian, Syrian, Greek, and Roman - will fall to Judah and Ephraim as they become one again in His Hand (Ezekiel 37 and Romans 11). His Kingdom will be restored upon this earth as it was in the very beginning with Adam. Yahweh will be our

God and our King and we will be His people. He will dwell face to face with us again!

Men of God, Bride of Yeshua, make yourselves ready to rule by His side. Run the race to win! Know that you are surrounded by a great cloud of witnesses, all the way back to Adam, cheering you on! Choose to wholeheartedly respond "yes" to His call to be His disciples in His Kingdom now so that you can stand united with Him in the fullness of His Kingdom then. Amen! (Hebrew: "So be it!")

Conclusion:
Now What?

In the past seven chapters, we've considered a wide range of "manhood in Yahweh's Kingdom" topics and concerns. I pray that you have made a positive response to Yeshua's personal call to you to become His disciple and begin stepping into all of the potential that He sees in you. You do not have to settle for any culture's status quo. You have so much more to become as a man in God's Kingdom. Yeshua knows that you have what it takes. If not, He would not have called out to you. His perception of you may be far different than how you see yourself right now. That does not matter! Who you can become is what matters most to him. You will have to trust His judgment, not your own and then go for it with gusto. Remember, He is right here with you and His very Breath (the Holy Spirit) will empower you to step up into the challenges before you and succeed.

As I bring a close to this book, I want to share with you one last personal story. I think you will be able to hear my heart as to why this topic of becoming a Real Man of God became and remains so very important to me.

The time was just over a decade ago. My youngest son, Matthew, was about 4 or 5 years old. Up to this time I had been raising my daughters with my second wife, Evelyn. (My first wife died of cancer, and Yahweh then blessed and honored me with this wonderful woman who now walks by my side.) Being a normal dad, I had been stumbling my way through raising girls with all of my triumphs and failures resting on my shoulders.

With Matthew, Yahweh began to open my eyes to things I had not seen about myself and about parenthood. Every day I would come home from work and this little fella would greet me as only he could. I was simply blown away by having a son to share my life with. Yet, as with my daughters before him, I knew that I was fumbling my way through the job of parenting a "boy child".

One day I was in the midst of reading and studying my Bible. I was looking at the life of David, King of Israel and slayer of lions, bears and giants. If you are familiar with the story, Yahweh comes to call David "a man after My own heart", which is remarkable since David was also an adulterer and murderer and not always the best at fatherhood. (One of his sons totally rebelled against him, attempting to dethrone and kill him.) Nonetheless, he loved Yahweh's Teaching and Instruction (the Torah). When confronted with his failures, he was quick to confess them and return to God's ways.

I came to the account of the end of David's life. Upon his deathbed, he called his son, Solomon, to his side. Solomon would soon be the new King of Israel. I am positive he was quite apprehensive as he came to hear what his dying father was going to say to him. David, being a Hebrew father, blessed his son, giving to him one last instruction.

The time had come for David to die; so he commissioned Solomon his son as follows:

"I am going the way of all the earth. Therefore, be strong; show yourself a man. Observe the charge of Yahweh your God to go in his ways and keep his regulations, commandments, rulings and instructions in accordance with what is written in the Torah of Moses; so that you will succeed in all that you do and wherever you go. If you do, Yahweh will fulfill what he promised me when he said, 'If your children pay attention to how they live, conducting themselves before me honestly with all their heart

and being, you will never lack a man on the throne of Israel.'"
I Kings 2:1-4

As I read this, I heard Father speak to my spirit, "Steve, raise your son to be this kind of a man."

I was taken back. I realized that based on what I had just read I had no idea how to raise a son – especially a son who would live honestly with all his heart and being before Yahweh, according to what was written in the Torah of Moses. As a disciple of Yeshua, I was only a couple of years into my walk of understanding and embracing the Hebrew perspectives and wisdom that He lived out on earth. How would I even begin to pass this on to my son?

Looking back, that moment in my life was also where this book and the program, Called to Be Men, was born. The actual concept had not yet crossed my mind, yet in my resulting studies on "how to raise a son according to Yahweh's teachings and instruction," it did not take me long to realize that for us Christian men, there was a huge gap in our upbringing and training to be Kingdom husbands and fathers.

Over the years following that day, I found in Yahweh's Word tremendous wisdom and practical instruction concerning how to raise my son and my daughters. I also found we could become people of honor, integrity, courage and faithfulness (fidelity). Not only could I and my children live as such before Yahweh, but we could also do so before our fellow man. Doing His will isn't spiritual guesswork! Yahweh has made His path very clear to His children. All we have to do is listen and obey.

As I learned, I began to look at the families, especially the husbands and fathers, surrounding me in the church and in my community. I became almost horrified at the serious damage our lack of knowledge and wisdom was doing. My brothers were in deep need of encouragement and help. Yahweh has so much better for us as men and has in place paths of blessings intended for our families. Yet, we are seriously missing the mark. I quickly came to understand that part of my ministry would one day entail getting this message out to as many men as possible.

Fast forward to today. We developed and started the program, Called to Be Men, in our congregation a few years ago. I was told by several ministers and many of the men who have gone through the instruction that it needed to be made into a book. So here it is – the book. Yet, I realize that even a good book and a solid program is still just the beginning for most men, including me. What do we do from here? How do we stay encouraged? How do we keep on growing into all of our God-given potential as men, husbands, and fathers? I have a few key steps for you to consider. You should definitely also ask Yahweh to lead you to other opportunities that will help you grow deeply in your Scripture-based understanding and walk as you become His Kingdom Man.

First, I encourage you to re-read this book as often as possible. Try the practical suggestions and try them more than once. If something feels uncomfortable, don't stop. Change takes time. Personally, I have found that understanding and becoming at ease in a new way of doing something comes only as I consistently put a wise instruction to use. This is true for every person, male or female.

Second, I also highly recommend that if there is a Called to Be Men program available to you in your location, sign up and go! You will meet other men there that are after the same things that you are; a better life, marriage, and home. You will also have the opportunity to ask questions, wrestle with the material, and ask for prayer as you start to make adjustments in response to what Yahweh gives to you in those sessions. If the Called to Be Men program isn't available, share this book with your pastor and ask him or her to consider bringing it to your church.

I also encourage you to go to church, men. Not just any church. Do your homework. Find a church that teaches ALL of the Bible, not just the New Testament. Find a congregation and pastor that embraces a Hebrew perspective in gaining insight and wisdom from the Word of God. If the pastor's preaching is stepping on your toes, it's not a bad thing. Don't settle for a constant diet of "feel good' messages that are more human philosophy than the Word of God. If you are to teach your children the Word of God, you must find a place where you are learning the Word of God yourself! As the spiritual head of your home, finding that church is your responsibility, not your wife's. Her input is very important and she needs to be involved in that decision. However, the responsibility of seeing to it that your family is being fed correctly by the church you become a part of, rests on your shoulders.

Get into reading and studying the Word of God on your own. Don't be intimidated by this. If it is the Hebrew perspective that you are after, I would suggest that you use a translation that has gone back to the Hebrew and has restored that perspective in its presentation. The Complete Jewish Bible is a good one, as is the One New Man translation. As you read the New Testament, pay attention to the cross-references. 85% of the New Testament can be found in the Old Testament, so use the cross references to help you go back and bring the wisdom and instruction of the Old Testament forward into your understanding of what the New Testament writers were attempting to say. If you really want to get serious, consider getting a good Hebrew-Greek study Bible that will help you get more accurate definitions from the original languages of the Word.

I cannot over emphasis the importance of studying Yahweh's Word, not only on your own but with other committed disciples of Yeshua. In fact, in the Hebrew world, it is the highest form of worship a person can give to Yahweh. We honor Him best by honoring His Word with our time and attention. One also never enters the House of Worship, a place of prayer and song, until he has first spent time in the House of Study. Yahweh is honored and pleased to see and hear His children reading and discussing His Word together. In the Hebrew world, the study of the Word of Yahweh always precedes what we today consider worship.

There is an old Hebrew adage that says, "Everybody needs a rabbi." I believe that is true! Find a good rabbi, a good teacher and mentor, of the Word of Yahweh, from a Hebrew perspective. It will help you considerably if your teacher has sound knowledge of the culture and traditions that grew out of the Hebrew love of the Torah. They can help you discern between what are truly Yahweh's instructions to us as His people and what are merely man-made tradition and practices. Many people are surprised at how simple and down to earth God's instructions truly are. Yeshua did say, "My yoke is easy and my burden is light." A good teacher will also be able to help you discover how to put God's instruction into practice day by day and keep you encouraged. As you learn how to rightly discern and then walk out His instructions, your life – especially your relationships - will be abundantly blessed.

Men, I also want to make you aware that if there is not a sound Hebrew roots congregation or teachers in your area, our congregation does provide online live-stream services that would be beneficial for both you and your family. We have our Shabbat services on a live-stream feed every Friday evening and Saturday afternoon for anyone to watch and receive instruction. We also live-stream some of our Tuesday evening studies. On our web site, you can also find other helpful resources that can be ordered and shipped directly to you. Our web site is www.elccmt.org.

Gentlemen, I want to encourage you with every ounce of passion in my bones to grab on to your Messiah, your Master Rabbi, and like Peter, determine that there is no one else to turn to but Him and no other place you can go but to be sitting at His feet being instructed and empowered by Him. Yahweh made a tremendous promise concerning the time that Yeshua would come to redeem and restore His people to Himself and to His Kingdom. That time came and is still here now.

> *"For this is the covenant I will make with the house of Israel [all who follow Yahweh] after those days," says Yahweh. "I will put my Torah within them and write it on their hearts; I will be their God, and they will be my people. None of them will teach his fellow-citizen or his brother saying, 'Know Yahweh!' For all will know me, from the least of them to the greatest, because I will be merciful toward their wickedness and remember their sins no more."* **Jeremiah 31:30-33 and Hebrews 8:10-12**

Almighty God's covenant, His Torah, is living inside of you! He placed it there through His Holy Spirit when you confessed your sins to Him and gave Yeshua the throne of grace-filled authority in your life. Yeshua IS the Living Torah and He is dwelling within you. To study His ways and follow them is already in you! In all honesty, as you study, all the Spirit really has to do is quicken what is already written on your heart. Obedience to His instruction and statutes will always be your wisest possible choice. His Ways are not difficult to comprehend or to walk in.

Our difficulties in obeying are usually not the instruction itself. Usually it is our own personal obstacles that stand in our way. Our struggle is found in leaving behind old habits and ways of thinking and doing things. Traditions and habits, good, bad, and sometimes downright evil, are handed down to us from generation to generation. Complicating this difficulty is the strong emotions that we tie to traditions and the warm memories that wrap around them. The instructions Yahweh gives to us truly are not difficult to do. It's the breaking off the emotional ties that we buck the hardest against. We have to trust Yahweh to help us see past the emotions and form new attachments to the rich Kingdom world He is giving to us. Believe me, it is so worth it.

I also know firsthand that when you begin to live out your choice to adjust to Yahweh's instructions, you feel like the whole world is scrutinizing you, especially close friends and family. In fact, friends and family can be a true test of your courage and faithfulness in following the Word. Some will even choose to cut you out of from their lives. This is when you need those who are walking a similar journey to be there for you, cheering you on. More significantly, this is when you need to confidently lean on the Holy Spirit to get you through to achieving what you know is right for you, your wife and your children. No matter how hard the challenge may be, Holy Spirit will not let you down. You will discover that those who know the Truth and the joy of walking with Yeshua will become closer than a brother to you. Do not lose heart!

Men, as disciples of Yeshua, we have it within us to be His men – constantly growing in courage, honor, fidelity and integrity. As we allow His Spirit to quicken His Word within us, we have every potential to become the husbands, fathers, and Godly influencers in our churches and communities Yahweh has designed and destined us to be. We are called to be HIS Men and the time is NOW to pick up the gauntlet and run this race to win! You can do this! I know you can – and most importantly, Yahweh knows you can!

The "Called to be Men" Declaration

"Yahweh our Elohim we will serve, and His voice we will obey."
Joshua 24:24

I declare on this day that, by diligence in the Word of Yahweh and the power of the Holy Spirit, I have chosen to be a Man of Honor in God's Kingdom.

As a Man of Honor
I will love Yahweh by obeying His Commandments with all my heart, all my soul, and all my strength.

As a Man of Honor
I will choose to take full responsibility for myself, my wife and my children. I will love and protect them, serve them. As the spiritual leader of my home, I will teach then the Torah of Yahweh.

As a Husband
I will be faithful to my wife. I will love and honor her, and be willing to lay down my life for her just as the Messiah did for me.

As a Father
I will teach my children to love Yahweh with all their heart, all their mind, and all their strength. I will teach them the Torah, as it is Truth for their lives. I will teach them to honor authority and to live a redeemed lifestyle.

As a Man of Honor
I will confront evil, pursue justice, and love mercy. I will treat others I desire to be treated: with kindness, respect and compassion.

As a Man of Honor

I will read Yahweh's Word daily, pray for others, and be faithful to my congregation.

As a Man of Honor

I will seek the face of Yahweh and walk in the principles of the Torah. I will honor Yahweh's Sabbath and His Feast Days.

As a Man of Honor

I will work diligently to provide for the physical, mental, and emotional needs of my family. I will honor my parents and teach my children to do the same.

As a Man of Honor

I will forgive others who have wronged me and be quick to reconcile with those that I have wronged.

As a Man of Honor

I will walk in integrity as a man answerable to Yahweh. I will speak truthfully and keep my promises.

Acknowledgements

I have had so much encouragement and help in building the program, Called to Be Men, and writing this book. So many wonderful people have given me the courage to create this God-ordained project. I wish to honor and thank them with all of my heart.

My deepest gratitude and honor to Yeshua my Messiah who has taught me by His Word and Spirit all that is now being passed on to you in this book of instruction. I believe with all of my heart that in its pages HE reveals HIS plan for men, husbands, and fathers for our time in history. In a culture that has done so much to damage manhood and a father's role in the home, Called to be Men, through timeless Biblical principles, restores and empowers male humans, to become true Godly men in thought and action.

I also want to honor and express loving gratefulness to my lovely wife, Evelyn, who has stood by me, believed in me, encouraged me, and fought for me and the visions Yahweh has given me to fulfill. She is my greatest encourager at home and in my ministry. She is Yahweh's greatest gift to me.

Yahweh has blessed me with remarkable relationships that I also want to acknowledge and honor. These men and women of the Most High have instructed and mentored me throughout the years.

I want to express my love and gratefulness to Everlasting Covenant Congregation in Billings, MT, for being the Body of Messiah that I have longed to be a part of. Each of you is a unique expression of Yeshua's best for us (Pastors Steve & Evelyn). Your love for us as ministers of His Gospel is a constant testimony of your belief in us. You are *family*. We love you so very much. It is your faithfulness to us that is a constant reminder of why you are worth pouring our lives into. Thank you for allowing us to be your pastors and teach you HIS ways by HIS Spirit!

Deepest gratitude is given to Rabbi Randy and Sandi Ludeman, Dr. Iglahliq Suuqiina of Indigenous Ministries International, and Chief Joseph Riverwind of Firekeepers International for being steadfast friends and mentors. You are always there to stand with me and provide the encouragement and exhortations so often needed by ministers of Yahweh's Gospel.

Last, but definitely not least, I want to thank my children and our grandchildren! Each of you are a priceless gift to my family and to the world. Your presence in my life is a constant reminder that Yahweh's Truth is my greatest legacy to you. May you each grow in your understanding of His Ways, and may you continue to increase in the blessing you are to the nations.

Pastor Steve Heimbichner
Billings, Montana 2019

About the Author

Pastor Steve Heimbichner has been in ministry since 1977. He ministered for eighteen years at the Montana Rescue Mission in Billings, Montana. He then served for twelve years as a chaplain for a national motorcycle group. He also traveled the United States for three years as an evangelist. In 2002, while living in Colorado Springs CO, he and his wife, Evelyn, were introduced to the Hebrew Roots of the Christian Faith. Since that time, they have been on an incredible journey of revelation and discovery in the Hebrew mindset and culture that has deepened their love for Messiah and given them a fiery passion for the Kingdom of Yahweh as taught and lived by Him. In 2006, Yahweh moved Steve and Evelyn back to Billings, MT to start a Hebrew Roots church called Everlasting Covenant Congregation. Since that time, they have continued to serve as pastors at ELCC ministering Truth to those hungry for Truth. In recent years they have also been blessed to be able to take the Hebrew Gospel of the Kingdom, through Called to be Men, to the Northern Cheyenne and Crow nations. Though Livestream broadcasts of ELCC's Shabbat services, Pastor Steve is also reaching into multiple locations across the United States and also into central Africa. Pastors Steve and Evelyn are anointed leaders who have a passion to take the Living Torah to the nations, empowering people to break free from their bondages and accomplish the unique destinies Yahweh has purposed for every individual.

Want to learn more about the crucial role of
Yeshua's Hebrew roots in your life?

Connect with us!

Pastor Steve Heimbichner
Everlasting Covenant Congregation
1304 Central Ave
Billings, Montana 59102

- **Website:** www.elccmt.org
- **Facebook:** "Like" and "Follow" our page!
Everlasting Covenant Congregation 1304 Central Ave
- **Golden Nuggets** – daily inspirational email
- Order the **Called to be Men video series**
- Join us on **Livestream** for our **Friday evening Shabbat services**
(www.livestream.com/accounts/14672578/events/4261976)
- **Visiting Billings Montana? Worship with us!**
- **Book as a guest speaker**
- **More Hebrew Roots resources are available on the ELCC website!**

Thank you for reading our book!

I really appreciate your feedback and I love hearing what you have to say.

I need your input to make the version of this book and my future books better.

Please leave me an honest review on Amazon, letting me know what you thought of the book.

Thank you so much!

--- Pastor Steve Heimbichner

www.ingramcontent.com/pod-product-compliance
Lightning Source LLC
LaVergne TN
LVHW011326080426
835513LV00006B/219